Revealed Treasures

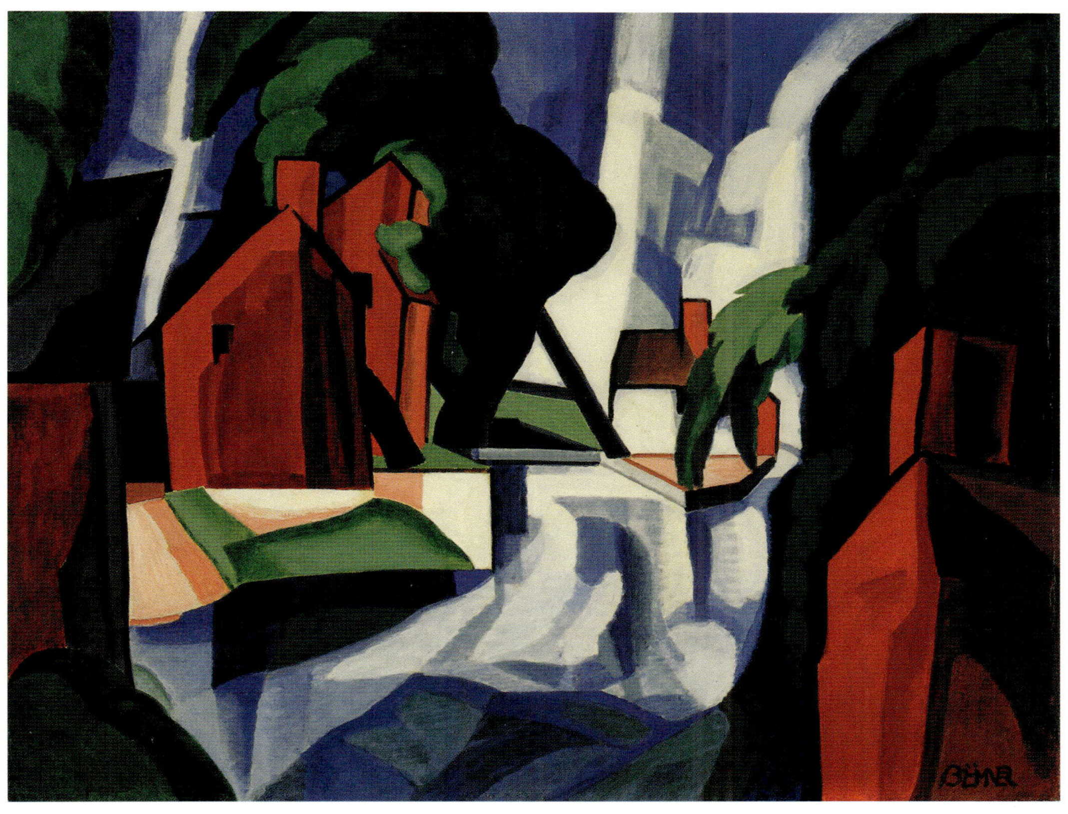

Drawings and Watercolors from the Amon Carter Museum

BY JANE MYERS
WITH SELECT ENTRIES BY SHIRLEY REECE-HUGHES

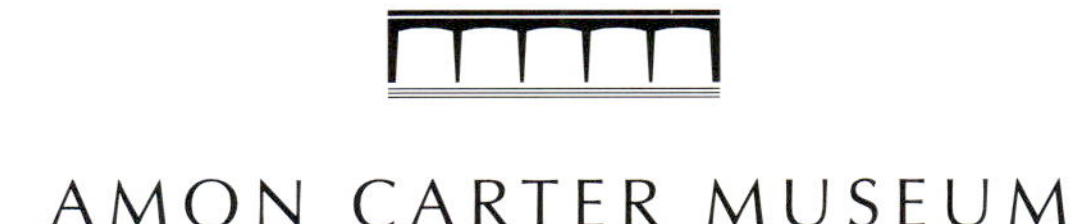

AMON CARTER MUSEUM

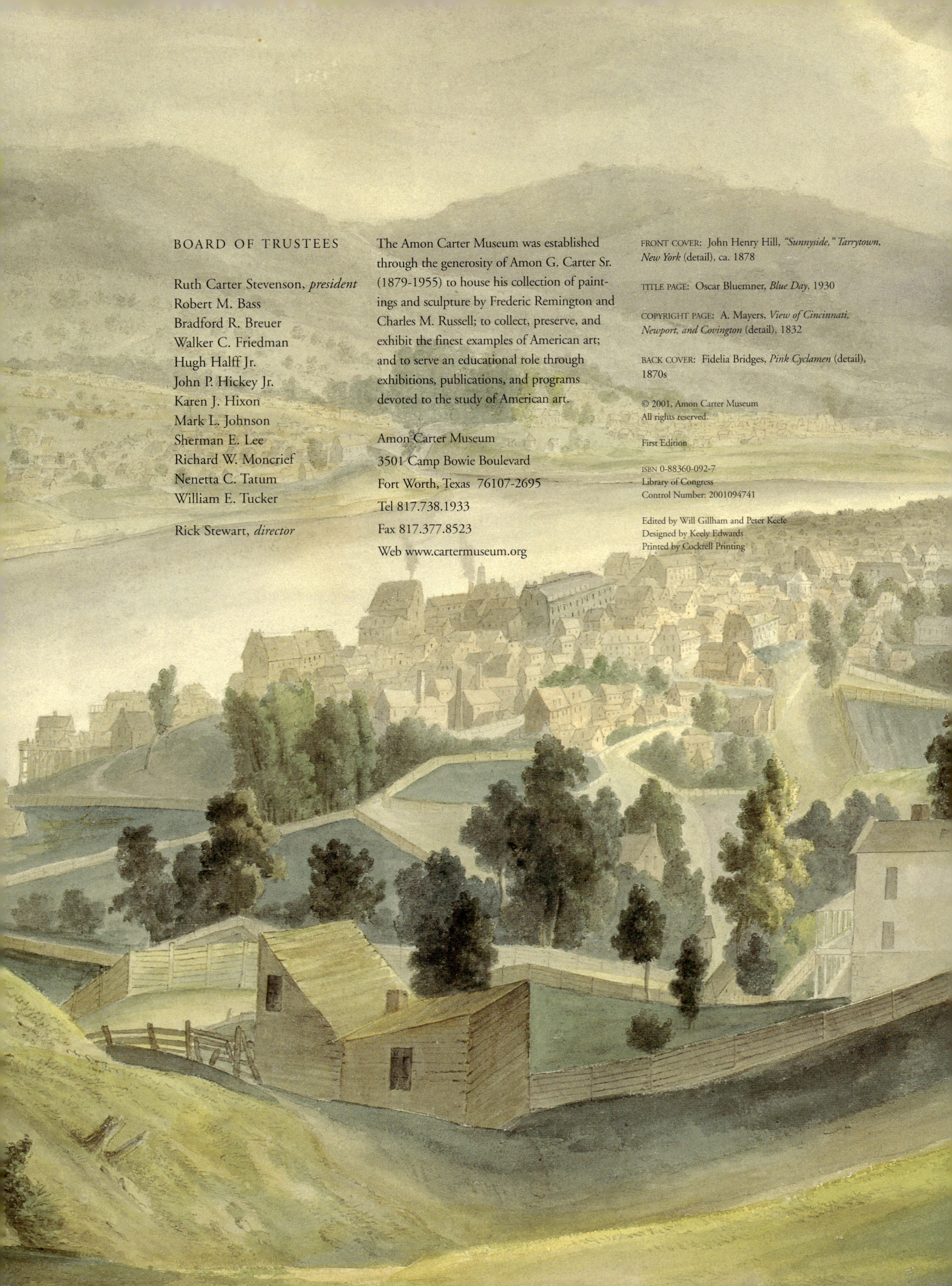

The Amon Carter Museum was established through the generosity of Amon G. Carter Sr. (1879-1955) to house his collection of paintings and sculpture by Frederic Remington and Charles M. Russell; to collect, preserve, and exhibit the finest examples of American art; and to serve an educational role through exhibitions, publications, and programs devoted to the study of American art.

Amon Carter Museum
3501 Camp Bowie Boulevard
Fort Worth, Texas 76107-2695
Tel 817.738.1933
Fax 817.377.8523
Web www.cartermuseum.org

FRONT COVER: John Henry Hill, *"Sunnyside," Tarrytown, New York* (detail), ca. 1878

TITLE PAGE: Oscar Bluemner, *Blue Day*, 1930

COPYRIGHT PAGE: A. Mayers, *View of Cincinnati, Newport, and Covington* (detail), 1832

BACK COVER: Fidelia Bridges, *Pink Cyclamen* (detail), 1870s

© 2001, Amon Carter Museum
All rights reserved.

First Edition

ISBN 0-88360-092-7
Library of Congress
Control Number: 2001094741

Edited by Will Gillham and Peter Keefe
Designed by Keely Edwards
Printed by Cockrell Printing

Foreword

The Amon Carter Museum's collection of watercolors and drawings began with Amon G. Carter Sr.'s purchase, in 1935, of nine watercolors by Charles M. Russell. The acquisition marked the beginning of Carter's renowned collection of western art. His collection grew over the next twenty years to form the core holdings of the Amon Carter Museum, the repository of American art that Carter had envisioned before his death in 1955.

Works on paper have continued to play a pivotal role in the growth of the collection. Shortly after opening in 1961, the museum began to embrace the broad American experience by extending the chronological and geographical range of the Carter's paintings, sculptures, and works on paper by Russell and Frederic Remington. This evolution is reflected in the works contained in this book, a group of forty-four masterworks of American draftsmanship, collected by the museum beginning in 1965 and spanning the period between 1791 and 1965. Each of these unique views, reflecting the artist's own time and place, conveys one facet of the rich, narrative fabric of American life.

The museum's mission to "collect, preserve, and exhibit the finest examples of American art" has been the driving force behind the development of the drawing and watercolor collection over the past forty years. Although perhaps a lesser-known aspect of the museum's superlative paintings, sculptures, photographs, and prints, the drawing collection has been shaped to parallel and augment these holdings. Works on paper build upon and enrich such strengths of the museum's collection as early westward exploration, American landscape and still life, and twentieth-century modernism. The earliest views of the American frontier as it moved relentlessly west were executed on paper, a readily transportable support. Euro-American artists provided rare views of both burgeoning urban communities along the western waterways, such as Cincinnati and Louisville, and the increasingly vestigial cultures of many of the West's indigenous peoples. By the second half of the nineteenth century, drawing came into its own as an independent means of self-expression. Representatives of the era's vanguard chose watercolor as their primary medium, including the American Pre-Raphaelites William Trost Richards, Fidelia Bridges, John William Hill, and Henry Roderick Newman. Highly personal expression and a fervor equal to the dawn of the modern age marked the works on paper of early-twentieth-century artists Georgia

O'Keeffe, John Marin, Charles Demuth, Arthur Dove, Oscar Bluemner, and Joseph Stella. Innovation continued into mid-century in the work of Charles E. Burchfield, William Fett, and Mark Tobey, whose watercolors represent the pinnacle of their artistic production.

A drawing's functional role provides fascinating insight into an artist's life, methods, and materials. Some sheets herein, such as those by James Goodwyn Clonney, James McNeill Whistler, and Stanley William Haseltine, were made as preliminary sketches for larger, finished oils. Other images were likely intended for broad distribution in the form of an etching or aquatint, including those by John H. B. Latrobe, A. Mayers, and James David Smillie. Still others were not only documentary but also scientific in origin, including the ornithological watercolors of John Abbot and the ethnographical works of Peter Moran. These drawings reflect the artists' comprehensive understanding of their craft as they made complex decisions—sometimes far from their studios—about translating value, light, and form to paper and, in so doing, leaving behind intimate traces of their perceptions. Selected as representative examples of the over 600 drawings and watercolors in the Amon Carter Museum collection, each of the following works provides a tantalizing slice of American art and history.

A number of generous donors have enabled the museum to acquire major works on paper. The collection has benefited greatly from the support of the Ruth Carter Stevenson Acquisitions Endowment and the Anne Burnett Tandy Accessions Fund. Generous individuals have donated works with noteworthy family provenances, including Mrs. Robert Johnson, Ruth Carter Stevenson, and Dr. Paola G. Zinnecker. The Council of the Amon Carter Museum provided the funds to acquire the pastels by James McNeill Whistler and Joseph Stella, as well as many other notable works of art since the group's formation in 1989.

The following colleagues provided invaluable information on the works discussed in this publication: Nancy Anderson, Linda Bailey, Marge Bardeen, Kathie Bennewitz, Libby Cluett, Geoffrey Dare, Sam Duncan, Nancy Finlay, Virginius C. Hall, Mary Sayre Haverstock, Susan A. Hobbs, Patricia Junker, Holly Krueger, Rebecca Lawton, Barney Lipscomb, Jane Posey, Kathleen Rice, John Rohrbach, Scott Fields, Kristin L. Spangenberg, Rick Stewart, Karin Strohbeck, Cathy Taylor, Stephanie Wiles, and the Williams Research Center of the Historic New Orleans Collection.

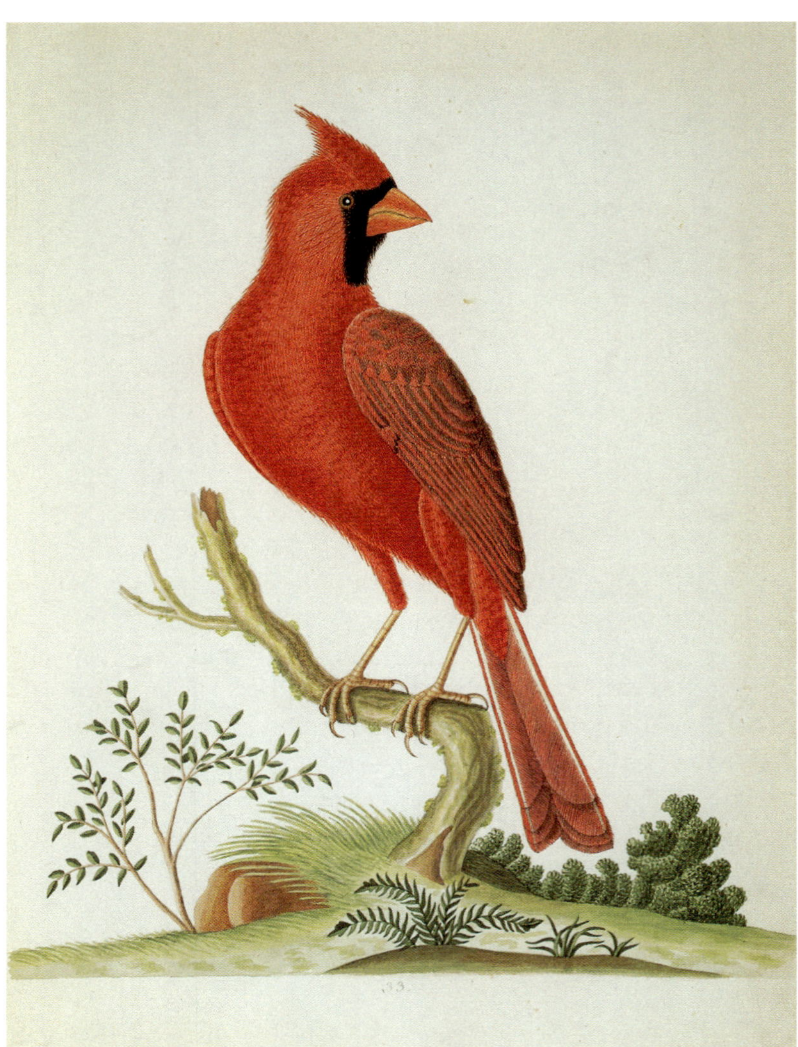

John Abbot
(1751–ca. 1840)

Cardinal Grosbeak (Loxia Cardinalis), 1791
Watercolor over graphite underdrawing on laid,
light blue paper mounted to wove paper
11¼ x 8¾ in. (28.5 x 22.2 cm)
Inscribed lower center: *.33.*
1980.51

Not all the English adventurers who risked the journey to the North American continent during the eighteenth century did so to cultivate the New World's fertile landscape. For some, like London-born John Abbot, who arrived in Virginia in 1773, the prospect of documenting the continent's abundant flora and fauna was ample enticement. With the rise of natural history as a scientific discipline, many Europeans eagerly sought out data on global plant and animal life, which they documented according to the scientific classification system devised by Swedish botanist Carolus Linnaeus.

In 1776, to avoid military activity surrounding the American Revolution, Abbot moved to Georgia, where he devoted the rest of his life to a comprehensive study of the birds, insects, and spiders of the Savannah River valley. Patrons paid him handsomely for his meticulous watercolors, as well as for the actual specimens that he collected and stuffed with cotton. These commissions were accompanied by the artist's detailed commentary on the habitats and behaviors of his subjects. Abbot's skill as a draftsman was highly respected by ornithologists, both in America and abroad, who admired his painstaking accuracy. To a graphite underdrawing, Abbot applied vivid watercolor, carefully delineating the feathers and other salient details with tiny brushstrokes that imparted delicate textures to the birds of Georgia, some of which are now extinct or endangered. The suggestion of a natural habitat through abbreviated and stylized motifs—such as the twisted miniature tree trunk on which this cardinal perches—reflects a popular pictorial convention of the period that helped a curious European clientele visualize the American terrain.

One of six ornithological watercolors by Abbot in the Amon Carter Museum's collection, *Cardinal Grosbeak (Loxia Cardinalis)* comes from an early group of the artist's commissioned work. Abbot's use of the Latin name in the title conforms to the Linnaean system, a categorization that helped legitimize the discipline of natural history. Now classified as *Cardinalis cardinalis*, the cardinal, admired for its brilliant plumage, was also recorded a few years later by John James Audubon during his travels in the American South.

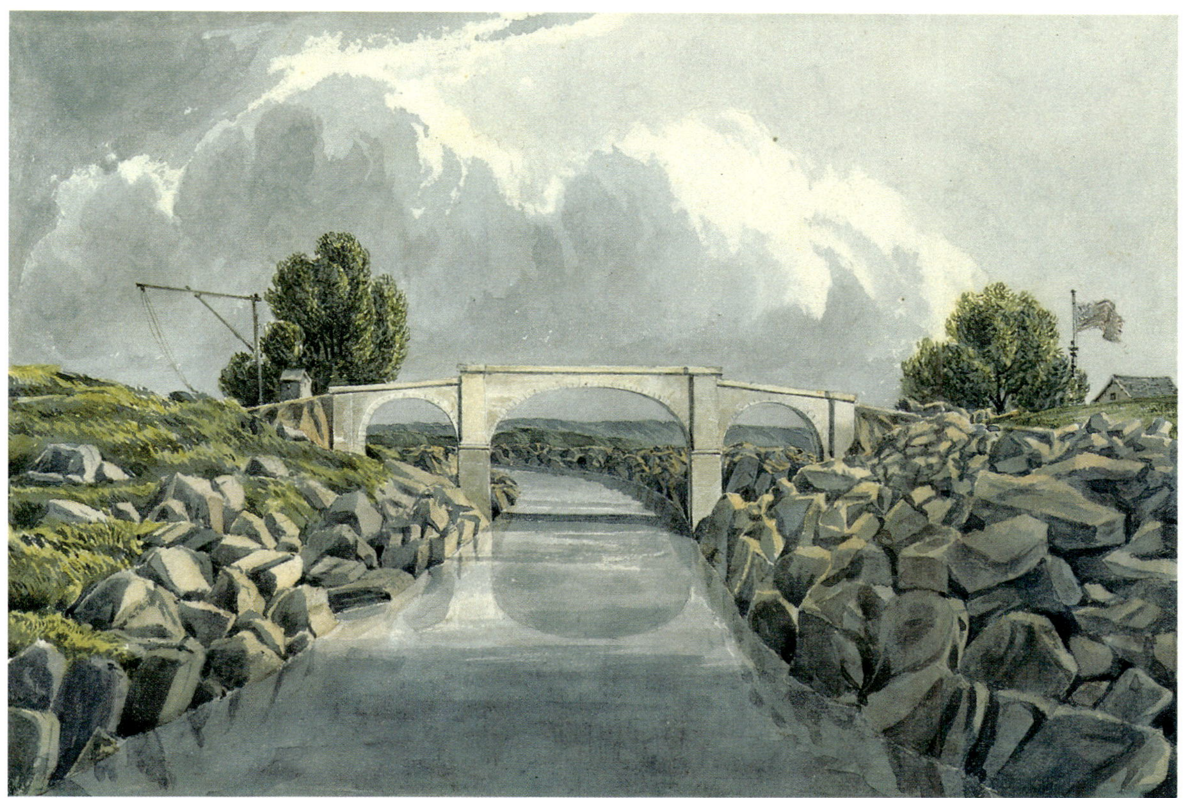

John H. B. Latrobe (1803–1891)

Canal Around the Falls of the Ohio, 1832
Watercolor over graphite underdrawing on wove, cream paper
7⅝ x 10⅝ in. (19.4 x 29.9 cm)
Inscribed lower center of margin: *Canal round the falls of Ohio*
1970.54

Ambitious and expensive feats of modern engineering, canals helped shape America during the 1820s and 1830s by overcoming natural obstacles to westward migration. The rapids on the Ohio River near Louisville, Kentucky, known as the Falls of the Ohio, rendered that mighty waterway nearly impassable, thus impacting the entire western river network. A limestone reef extending across the river virtually halted travel during periods of low water levels, when travelers with their goods were forced to portage around the Falls.

During one of his frequent western excursions, John H. B. Latrobe, a lawyer from Baltimore, stopped to observe the arched bridge that crossed the two-mile Louisville and Portland Canal, built in 1830 to bypass the Falls. In his diary, Latrobe marveled at the perfection of the design and the quality of its masonry. His comments reflect the exacting standards of his father, architect and engineer Benjamin Latrobe, who, although most famous for his designs for the U.S. Capitol and Baltimore Cathedral, was also highly regarded for his expertise in bridge and canal design.

Like his father, Latrobe was a proficient draftsman who employed a system of tonal modulations to indicate light and shade, later adding local color to describe the foliage and sky. Latrobe had reproduced similar drawings as color aquatints in Lucas Fielding's important landscape drawing manual, *Lucas' Progressive Drawing Book…Consisting Chiefly of Original Views of American Scenery* (1827–28). Indeed, inscriptions on the verso of this sheet and the other four watercolors by Latrobe in the Amon Carter Museum's collection indicate that this group was intended for yet another, apparently unrealized, compilation of printed views.

For Latrobe, the canal around the Falls of the Ohio represented an ingenious application of technical knowledge that enabled Americans to circumvent a barrier to economic and commercial settlement of the frontier. Ironically, as counsel for the Baltimore & Ohio Railroad for sixty years, Latrobe contributed to the rise of a mode of transportation that soon outpaced America's canal system of thoroughfares.

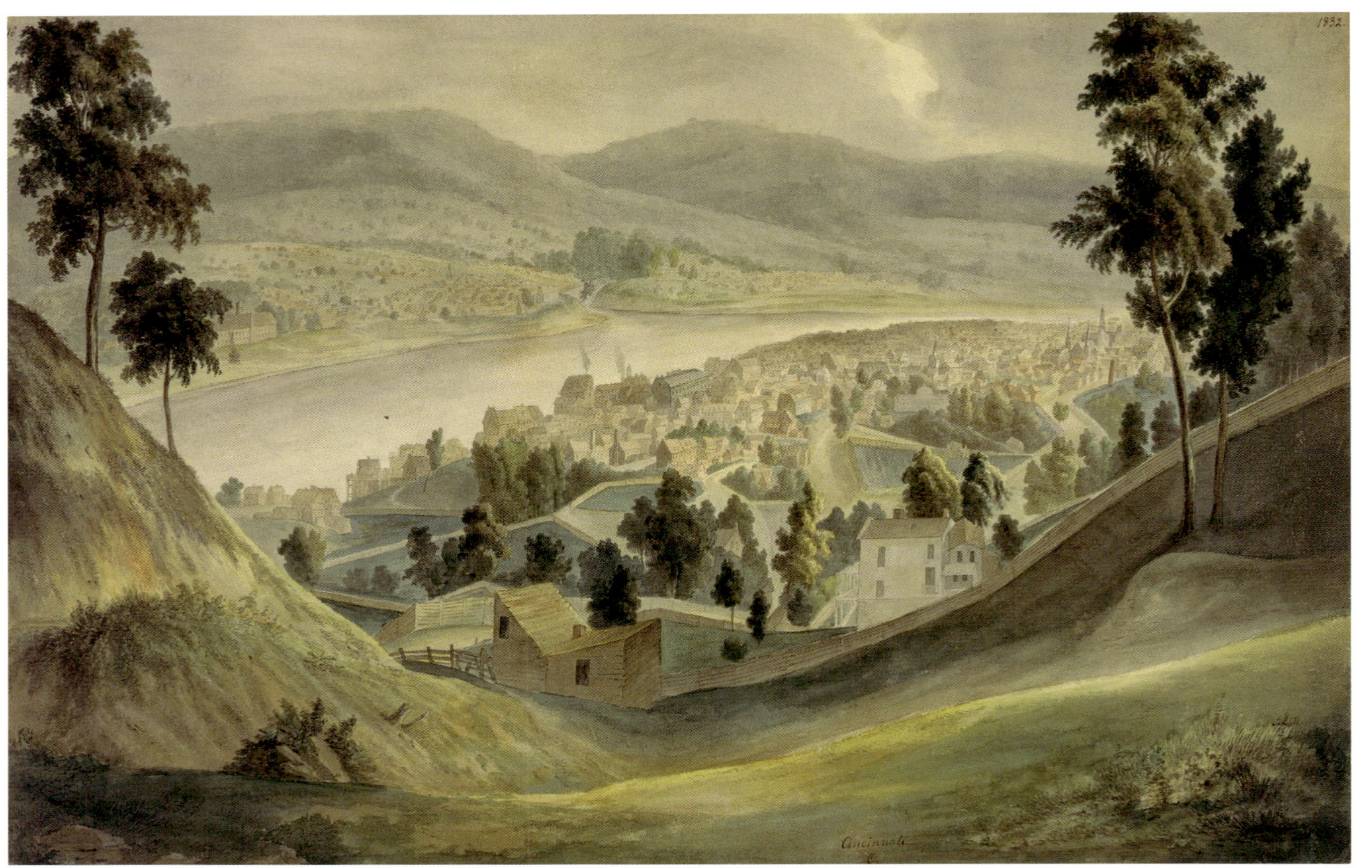

A. Mayers (active ca. 1832)

View of Cincinnati, Newport, and Covington, 1832
Watercolor and graphite on wove, off-white paper
12⅛ x 19⅛ in. (30.8 x 48.5 cm)
Signed, dated, and inscribed, upper left: *No 16*; upper right: *1832.*; lower center: *Cincinnati/O.*; on reverse, center: *A. Mayers.*;
lower left: *Vue de cincinnati, Newport et covington/O. KY.*
1974.19

Founded in 1788 on the banks of the majestic Ohio River, Cincinnati in the early 1830s was the preeminent frontier boomtown, developing rapidly as a center of transportation and industry. The town's burgeoning economy and emerging cultural and intellectual community attracted not only Americans gravitating west—such as the family of twenty-one-year-old Harriet Beecher (later Stowe) who moved there in 1832—but also Europeans, such as Frances Trollope, the British doyenne generally critical of American manners who lived there from 1828–30, and French writer and statesman Alexis de Tocqueville who visited in 1831. All praised the natural beauty of the site and commended its palpable energy and boundless potential.

A Parisian drawing master, A. Mayers arrived in Cincinnati during the summer of 1832. His work as a topographical painter is known only by seven watercolors—all of which reside in the Amon Carter Museum's collection—that he executed of Cincinnati and its environs. Mayers created this view with a draftman's accuracy, illustrating the city's advantageous location nestled between gently sloping hills. Across the river lie the two Kentucky communities, Newport and Covington, separated by the Licking River. Mayers tinted his drawing using soft colored washes; the tonalities gradually decrease in intensity toward the background, where they dissolve to faint blue, pink, and green. This limited color range, as well as the numbers inscribed on the upper-left corner of each of the seven sheets, suggests that the artist intended to turn his watercolors into a portfolio of delicate, landscape aquatints, which were fashionable at the time.

In addition to providing art lessons, Mayers established an art gallery in Cincinnati featuring his own paintings along with Chinese artifacts. Perhaps dispirited by the cholera epidemic of 1832, the artist apparently followed the Ohio and Mississippi Rivers to New Orleans, moving on like so many of the country's young, ambitious citizens pursuing their dreams in the New World.

Francis Blackwell Mayer (1827–1899)

The Thunder or Round Dance, 1857

Transparent and opaque watercolor and graphite on wove, cream paper
11⅞ x 15¼ in. (30.2 x 38.7 cm)
Signed and dated, lower left: *F. B. Mayer 1857*; lower right: *F. B. Mayer*
Purchase with funds provided by the Anne Burnett Tandy Accessions Fund
1992.2

In the summer of 1851, young Baltimore artist Francis (Frank) Blackwell Mayer eagerly seized an opportunity to observe Native American culture in the Upper Midwest. He accompanied the U.S. commissioners charged with conducting treaty negotiations at Traverse de Sioux, a trading post and village in the Minnesota Territory. There, over a period of several weeks, Mayer witnessed the activities of several thousand Dakota gathered for a treaty council.

The rainy season, during which the Native Americans assembled, occasioned the thunder, or round, dance, one of many scenes the artist recorded in his diary and sketchbook. Red, bird-like forms cut from bark and suspended from four saplings signify the noisy creatures thought to be responsible for thunder. The medicine man, beating on a drum, sits in the center of the assembly, encircled by an arbor of bushes, chanting men and women, and warriors on horseback. Shortly after this ceremony took place, the parties signed the historic treaty whereby the Dakota ceded their land and relocated to a reservation.

Like Alfred Jacob Miller, one of his artistic mentors in Baltimore who had visited the Rocky Mountains in 1837, Mayer anticipated finding a market for his works and in 1857 made this finished watercolor from his field sketches. The artist never succeeded in financially capitalizing on his western sojourn, yet the image of the thunder dance gained currency when it was published in Henry Rowe Schoolcraft's multivolume opus, *Historical and Statistical Information Respecting the History, Condition, and Prospects of the Indian Tribes of the United States* (1851–57).

After his trip to the Minnesota Territory, Mayer's interest in the West never waned; at the time of his death, he was working on a series of watercolors based on his Minnesota sketches for the noted Baltimore collector Henry Walters. The future of the Dakota was less sanguine. Relocation rendered their farming economy useless, leading to warfare with settlers and forever erasing their traditional way of life.

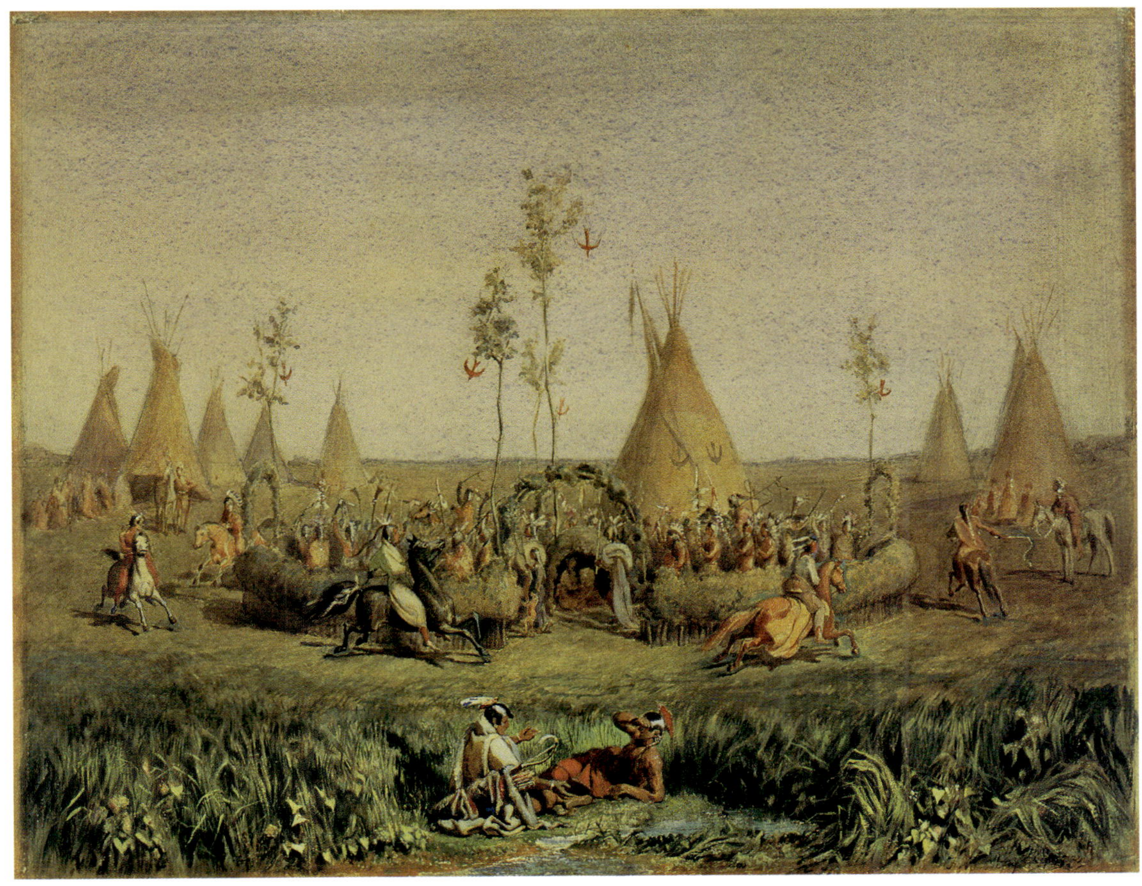

James Goodwyn Clonney
(1812–1867)

Study of a Man, 1842
Watercolor and graphite on wove, buff paper
11⅝ x 5⅜ in. (29.5 x 13.7 cm)
Signed and dated lower right: *Clonney/1842*
1983.150

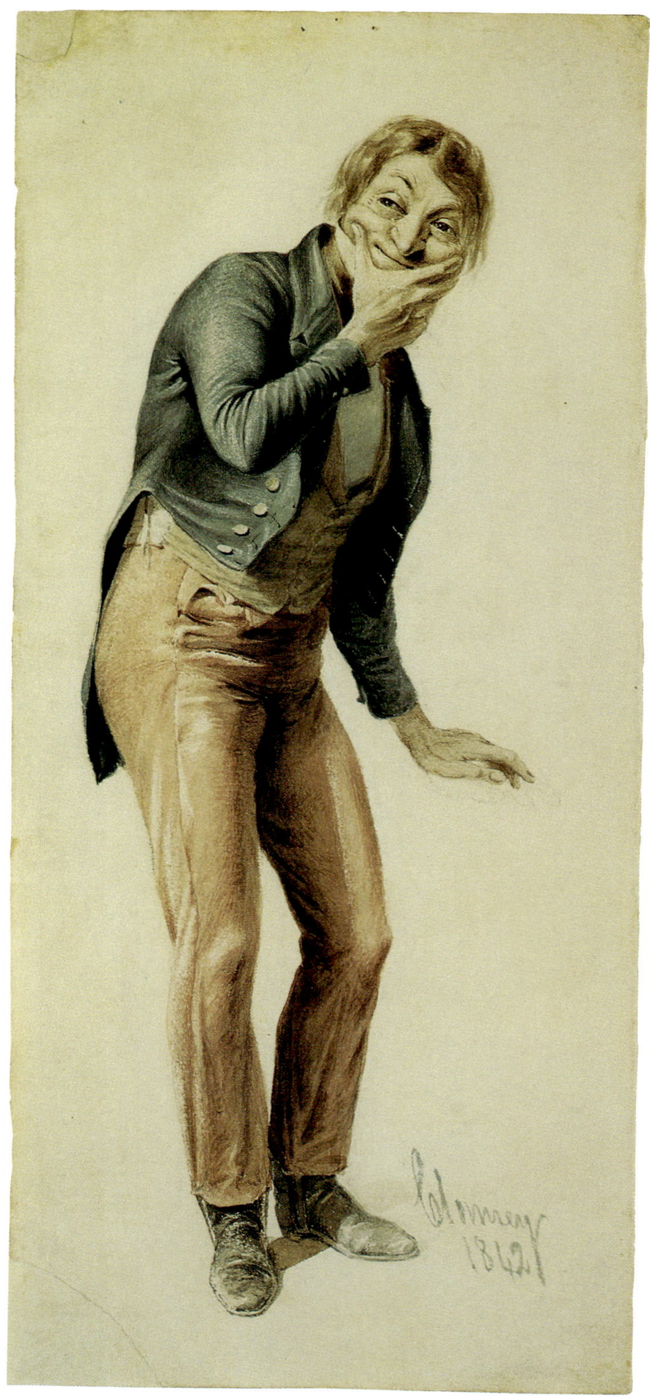

James Clonney, one of America's earliest genre painters, carefully planned his oil paintings by first making detailed watercolor drawings and then transferring them precisely to canvas. Clonney may have executed this lively drawing in preparation for a lost painting, possibly *Jonathan's Introduction into Good Society,* exhibited at the National Academy of Design in New York in 1842. An oil sketch for the painting (Museum of Fine Arts, Boston) relays a humorous narrative set in a drawing room, where a bumpkin, Jonathan, responds inappropriately to a statue of Venus while a more sophisticated suitor woos a young woman.

Clonney's figure represents a popular character type of the Jacksonian era. With the rise of democracy, the contrast between the general populace and the educated elite became a favorite humorous conceit. This bumbling, vernacular figure came to stand for the archetypal American common man. Clonney employed deft touches to capture the eccentricities of his character: long, disheveled hair; a wrinkled tailcoat, which challenges contemporary fashion by being too small; and scuffed shoes, an effect the artist produced by carefully scraping out the pigment. Evidence that the gesture of the slightly exaggerated left hand was altered indicates the artist's precise deliberations before the transfer to canvas. The figure's tilted posture suggests that in the final painting he was intended to lean on a table or other means of support. With a few precise strokes of the brush, the artist captures the spontaneity of the figure's momentary expression of bemusement as he cups his chin in his hand, arches his brow, and slyly smiles, his large nose adding another distinguishing detail to the caricature. Clonney also works out a simple palette, gently modeling the figure with light watercolor washes of blue, brown, and red.

Little is known about Clonney's artistic training. Born in England, he was living in New York by 1830 and working for a lithography firm. Like other artists of the period, including George Caleb Bingham and William Sidney Mount, he gravitated to genre painting. Between 1834 and 1852 he exhibited his work frequently, finding a sympathetic audience for his interpretations of contemporary life.

Jacob Maentel
(1778 – 1863)

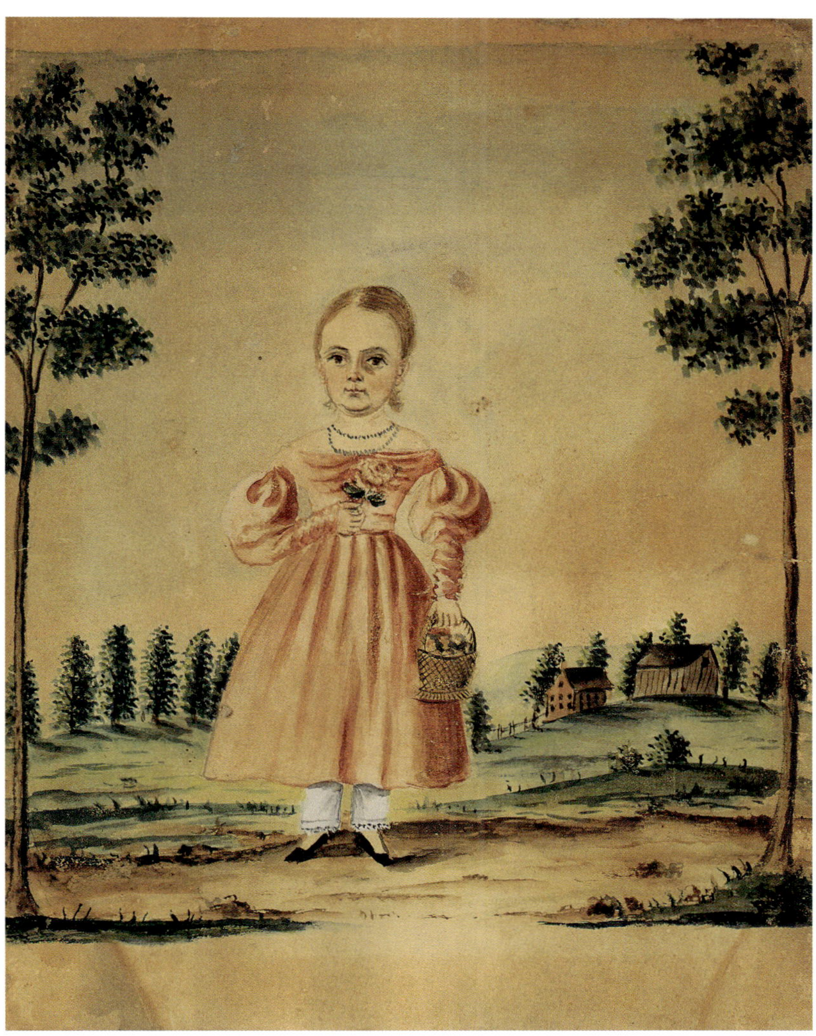

Portrait of Emma Louise Koser, ca. 1853
Transparent and opaque watercolor on wove, tan paper
9⅞ x 7⅞ in. (25.1 x 20 cm)
Gift of Mrs. Robert Johnson
1997.159

Even with the advent of photography, the most common type of middle-class portraiture in the mid-nineteenth century was the work of itinerant painters, generally untrained artists who traveled the countryside in search of patrons. Around 1855, Jacob Maentel was commissioned to paint this portrait of Emma Louise Koser, the young daughter of a cabinet and coffin maker in Mount Carmel, Illinois. Maentel had followed the tide west in 1838, settling with his family in New Harmony, Indiana, not far down the Wabash River from the Koser's community on the other side of the waterway.

Maentel, who had emigrated from Germany in 1806, came to southwestern Indiana after a profitable career as a watercolor portraitist in Lancaster County, Pennsylvania. He presents young Emma here in a straightforward pose that emphasizes her silhouette against the faintly articulated sky. Executed toward the end of Maentel's career, this delicate watercolor bears the hallmarks he successfully replicated throughout his long career: a farm designated by a house and barn in the distance; the girl's single rose and basket; her tiny, blue-beaded necklace; the linear pattern created by the folds of her dress and puffed sleeves; the landscape recession in parallel, linear planes; and a distinctive row of evenly spaced trees marking the terminus of the pictorial space. Despite his repetition of such dependable formulas, Maentel faithfully evoked Emma's individualized and salient features, including her wide, dark eyes and well-formed chin, as confirmed by a photograph of her made decades later.

This watercolor contradicts the frustrating propensity for folk portraits to be dissociated from the lives of their often anonymous subjects. Here, one has the satisfaction of knowing that Emma enjoyed a full life; she married John Nelson Johnson, the owner of a furniture store in his native Mount Vernon, Illinois, and lived into her mid-nineties. A true family keepsake, this portrait remained in the possession of her descendants until 1997, when they entrusted it to the holdings of the Amon Carter Museum.

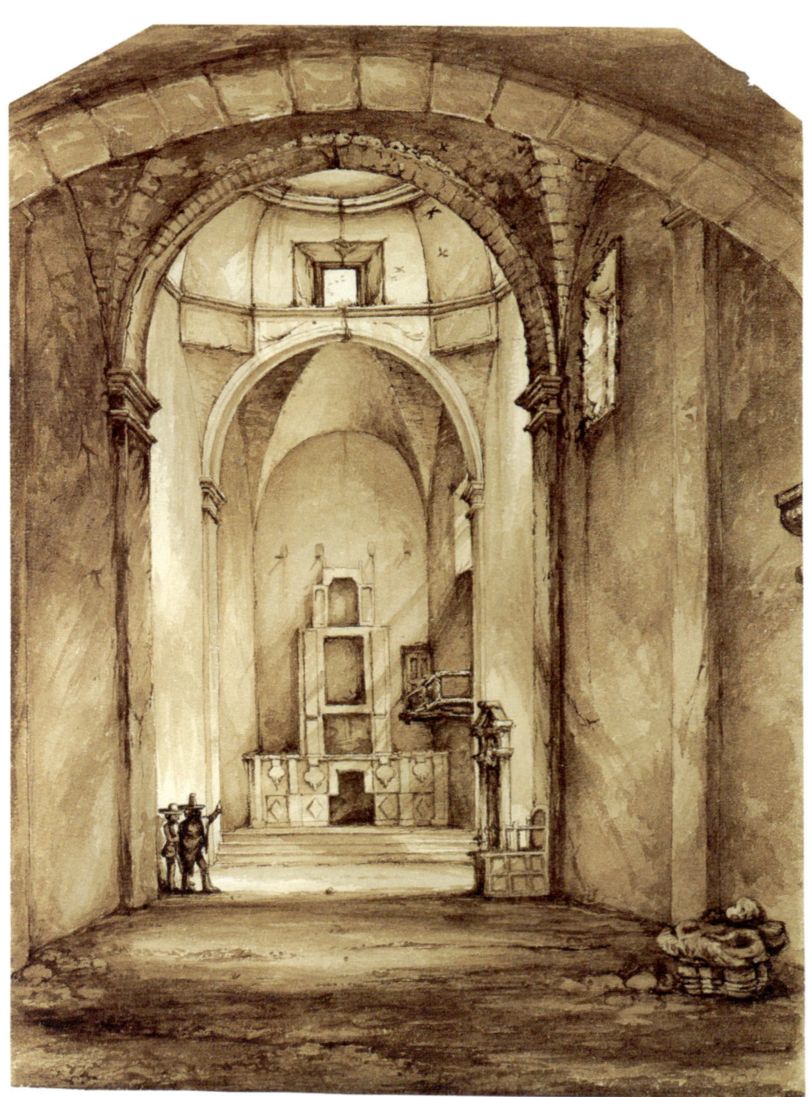

James Gilchrist Benton
(1820 – 1881)

Interior of Church, San José, ca. 1852
Ink and ink wash on wove, off-white paper
$10^{7}/_{8}$ x $8^{3}/_{16}$ in. (27.6 x 20.8 cm)
Inscribed on reverse, lower left to
lower right: *Interior of Church, San José*
1999.25.16

San José y San Miguel de Aguayo was the largest of five missions established along the San Antonio River in Texas in the wake of Spain's colonial expansion, which was centered on the conversion of the region's indigenous peoples to the Catholic faith. Founded in 1720, the San José mission served as a social and cultural center for several hundred Coahuiltecan and other indigenous peoples, whom the missionaries trained in the basic skills of farming and cattle raising. The thick walls and heavy buttresses of the mission church, completed in 1782, provided a strong fortification for the community against occasional raids from hostile Apaches.

Lieutenant James Gilchrist Benton, a New Hampshire native and graduate of West Point, made this ink and wash drawing of the church's interior while stationed in San Antonio. No longer an active mission and periodically occupied by the military, the building had deteriorated over its seventy-year history. This view looks down the nave's masonry vault toward the sanctuary, where there stands a wooden altarscreen decorated with carved relief panels and niches empty of their devotional icons. Daylight through several small windows casts shadows across the interior; the high, central opening marks the building's distinctive hemispherical dome at the junction of the nave and the transept. This refined sensitivity to detail, light, shadow, and perspective reflects Benton's training at West Point, where he learned documentary, topographical draftsmanship.

Interior of Church, San José is one of eighty-eight sheets from an album containing other views rendered by Benton in and around San Antonio, including Mission San Antonio (the Alamo), scenes of everyday life, and early Hispanic domestic architecture, as well as scenes from Benton's travels throughout the southern United States. Newspaper accounts suggest that the artist's Texas images may have been used to create one of the giant moving panoramas that captivated audiences in the 1840s and early 1850s. Said to be 300 feet in length, the panorama was assembled in New Orleans and featured scenes, including the battle of the Alamo, from California and Texas—two states that held abundant romantic and exotic appeal in America's popular imagination.

William Stanley Haseltine (1835–1900)

Indian Rock with Two Fishermen, Narragansett Bay,
Rhode Island, ca. 1862–63
Ink, ink wash, and graphite on wove, cream paper
$15\frac{1}{8}$ x 22 in. (38.4 x 55.9 cm)
Signed lower right: *W. S. H.*
1983.133

William Stanley Haseltine's fascination with Indian Rock, a mound of heavily fissured red granite on Rhode Island's Narragansett Bay, resulted in some of his first artistic achievements. During the early 1860s, Haseltine traveled the New England coastline, making magnificent ink and graphite studies for a series of oil paintings. Deftly applying ink to paper, Haseltine probed the shadow, volume, and texture of this singular rock, which, according to legend, was stained red from the spilled blood of Native Americans.

In this rendering, Haseltine chose an unusual perspective that obscures the rock's characteristic monolithic contours. Tiny ripples indicate the rock's watery surroundings, while two, lightly sketched fishermen reveal its scale. The shoreline, a sweeping compositional armature, radiates from the craggy focal point and recedes in a great curve south toward the Atlantic Ocean, where it merges with a delicately drawn horizon line defined by the sails of two distant ships. Haseltine's emphasis on line combines with the ink washes to define the rigid facets of stone. This keen sense of geologic accuracy reflects the rising interest in the earth sciences at this time and the contemporary taste for exacting natural effects. By alluding to a powerful geologic force, Haseltine expresses here the scientific curiosity he pursued as a student at Harvard University. His style reflects his training at the Düsseldorf Academy, where he studied for several years during the 1850s; his emphasis on sharp delineation, accuracy, and isolated natural components was part of the curriculum at Düsseldorf, which had attracted many American landscape students earlier in the century.

In 1866 Haseltine moved to Europe, eventually settling in Rome, his primary residence for the remainder of his life. There, he continued to portray the conjunction of water and land in both watercolors and large-scale oil paintings that attracted the patronage of American travelers.

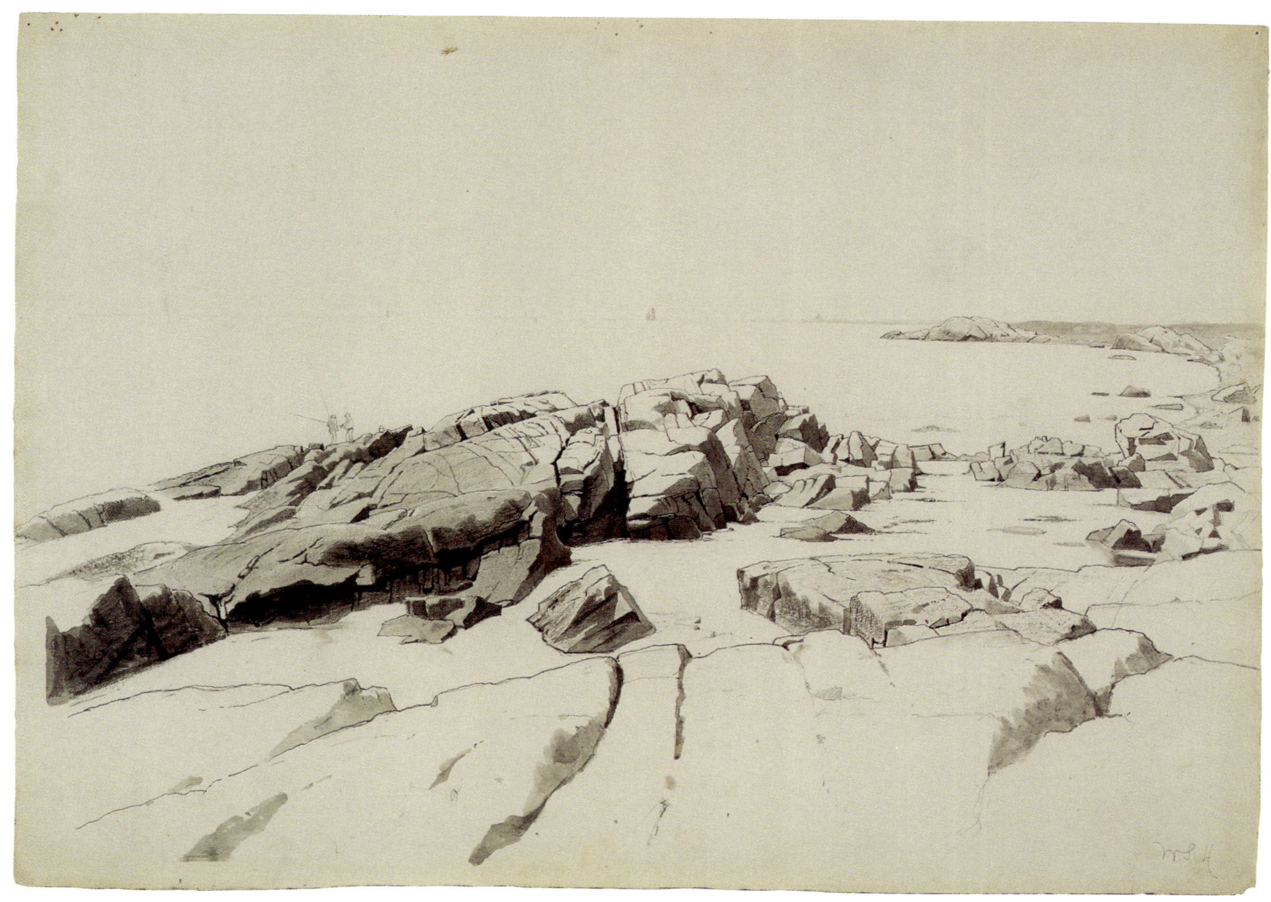

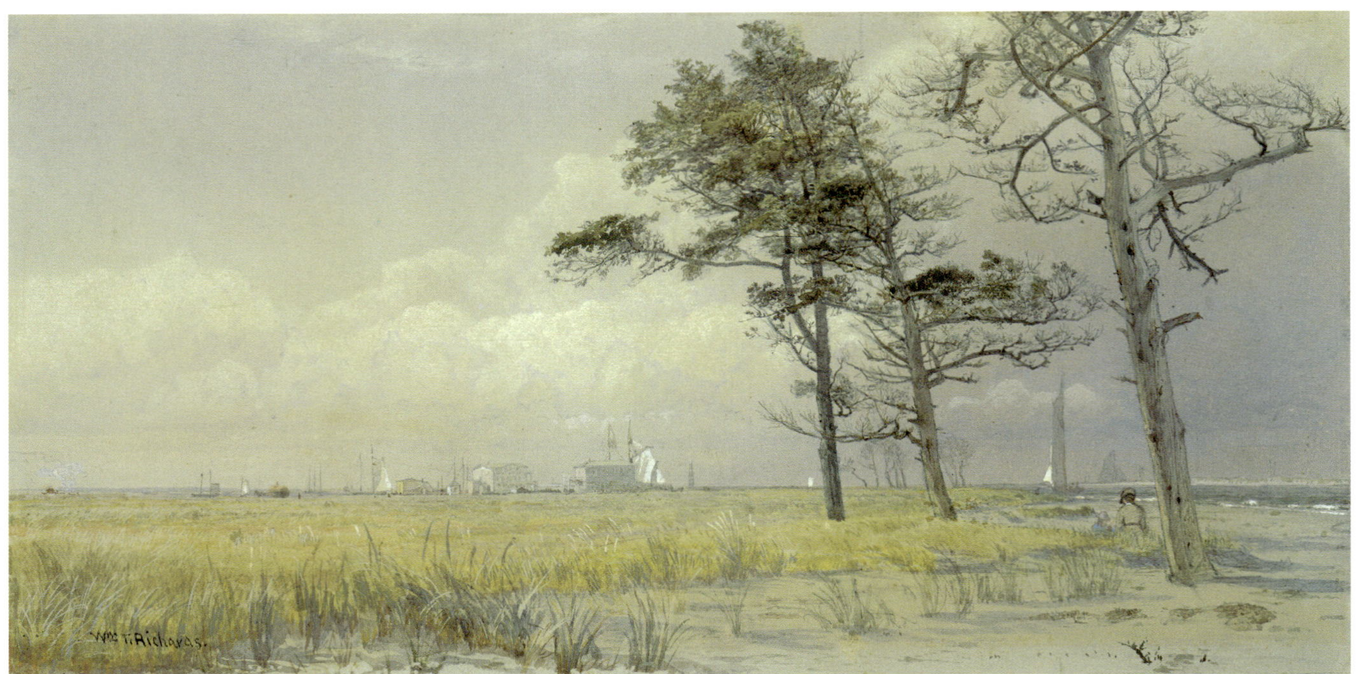

William Trost Richards (1833–1905)

Salt Meadows, Atlantic City, New Jersey, ca. 1871–73
Transparent and opaque watercolor on wove, gray paper
6⅞ x 14 in. (17.4 x 35.6 cm)
Signed and inscribed, lower left: *Wm T. Richards*; on reverse, lower right: *Salt Meadows/Atlantic City*
1984.37

Momentous changes in the country's transportation system during the mid-nineteenth century made more convenient and inexpensive travel possible for artists seeking to explore new locales for landscape subjects. Their destinations were often dictated by improved access to developing resorts, such as Atlantic City, New Jersey, whose entrepreneurs began to lure travelers in the years leading up to the Civil War. Within a few hours, William Trost Richards could reach Atlantic City from his Germantown, Pennsylvania, home, some sixty miles distant. When the artist painted this view in the early 1870s, the popular recreational area was attracting thousands of tourists seeking to escape the urban summer heat in favor of fishing, bathing, gambling, and other amusements.

This languid view of the distinctive salt marshes along the coastline, one of many watercolors Richards made near Atlantic City, marked a new breadth in the artist's style. Beginning in the late 1850s, Richards, a devotee of the writings of English critic John Ruskin, produced in exacting detail highly finished watercolor nature studies. As the influence of this aesthetic movement waned toward the end of the 1860s, however, Richards shed sharp clarity for a more evocative and distant view of the landscape.

In this work, a transparent blue wash produces the subtlest of tinted gradations, creating, in combination with the pale gray paper, an overall, unified tonality. Richards coupled this interest in atmosphere with his earlier penchant for minute details by denoting signs of the landscape's human inhabitants: two figures relaxing beneath the tree to the right, sailboats, and assorted buildings hugging the horizontal line that separates sky and earth. Trees, grasses, sails, and the waves gently lapping against the shore suggest gentle movement within a suspended moment on a tranquil summer day.

Such scenes of the Atlantic coast helped establish Richards as a major watercolorist of the 1870s. When shown in New York, his works were lauded for their delicacy and conformance to truthful representation.

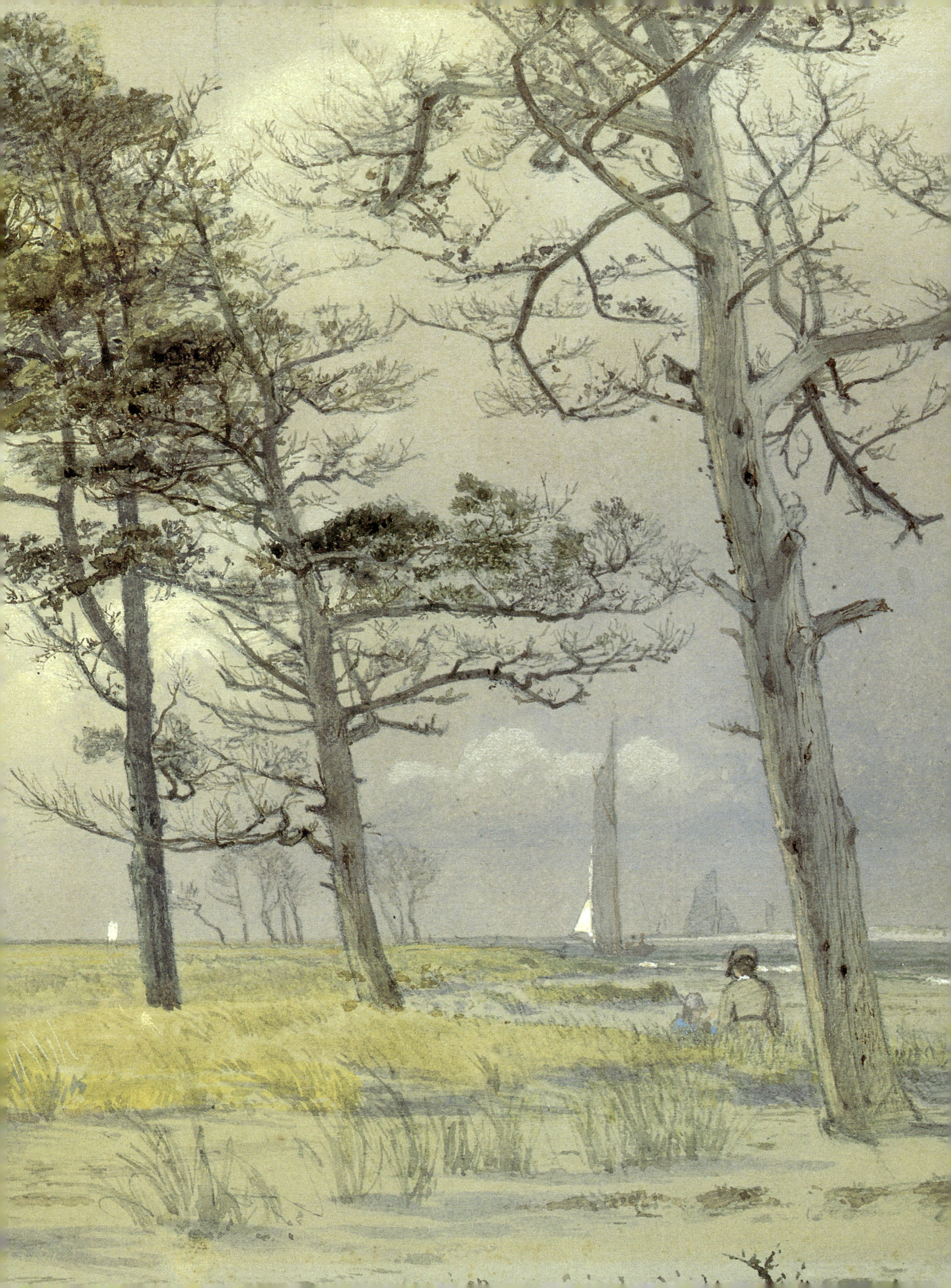

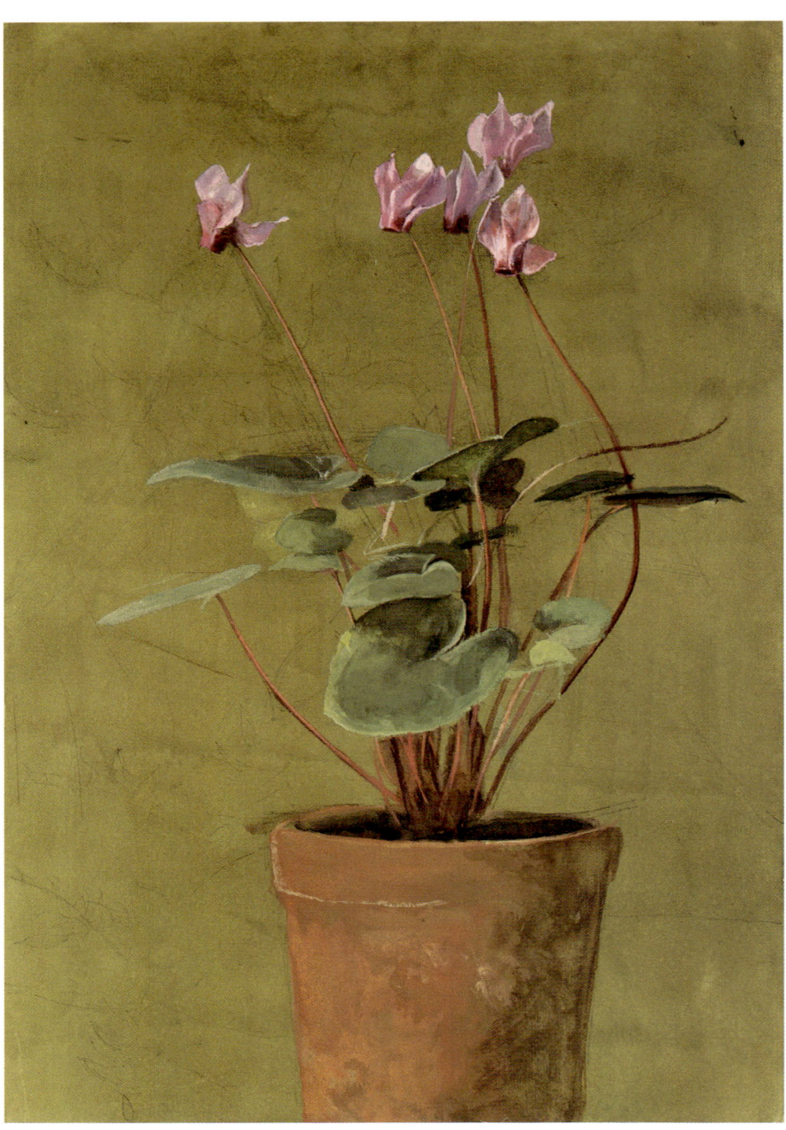

Fidelia Bridges
(1834–1923)

Pink Cyclamen, 1870s
Opaque watercolor and graphite on wove, light green paper
14 x 10 in. (35.6 x 25.4 cm)
1982.49

A host of romantic, aesthetic, and symbolic associations made flowers one of the few sanctioned themes for nineteenth-century women artists. The floral still lifes of Fidelia Bridges reflect her involvement with the American Pre-Raphaelite artists through her mentor, William Trost Richards. She met Richards in Philadelphia in 1860 when she moved there from Brooklyn to study at the Pennsylvania Academy of the Fine Arts. The American Pre-Raphaelites, whose leading adherents also included John Henry Hill and Henry Roderick Newman, flourished during the late 1850s and 1860s, making crisply detailed watercolor landscapes and still lifes.

Bridges frequently chose to show plants at close range, set within a landscape backdrop. She produced such views during summers in Connecticut, where she could indulge her love of the outdoors by spending long stretches of time painting birds and wild flowers. *Pink Cyclamen* is an emphatically domesticated variant of the American Pre-Raphaelites' penchant for nature studies. Although Bridges had traveled to Europe in 1867–68, her subject matter remained circumscribed by her immediate surroundings;

perhaps this cyclamen, a plant that blooms in the cooler months, brightened her apartment or studio in Brooklyn. The artist calls attention to the plant's intrinsically elegant design by setting it against a flat green background, while the heart-shaped leaves and sinuous stems, topped by pink and magenta blossoms, create a graceful ballet as the plant nods toward the daylight.

Such expressive, somewhat anthropomorphic, overtones may have reflected society's general fascination with flowers' emblematic meanings. Books adapted from the European "language of flowers," with individual meanings for each flower imparted through image and text, were well established within the culture, while contemporary poetry extolled the cyclamen's delicate petals for evoking a lover's lips. Another gender association was the appearance of cyclamen in medical manuals of the period as a remedy for various aliments unique to women. Such potent ties to femininity add a poignant dimension to Bridges' depiction of this isolated plant. Although the artist loved children and had supported herself by working as a governess, she never married and frequently lamented the lonelier aspects of her days.

James McNeill Whistler
(1834–1903)

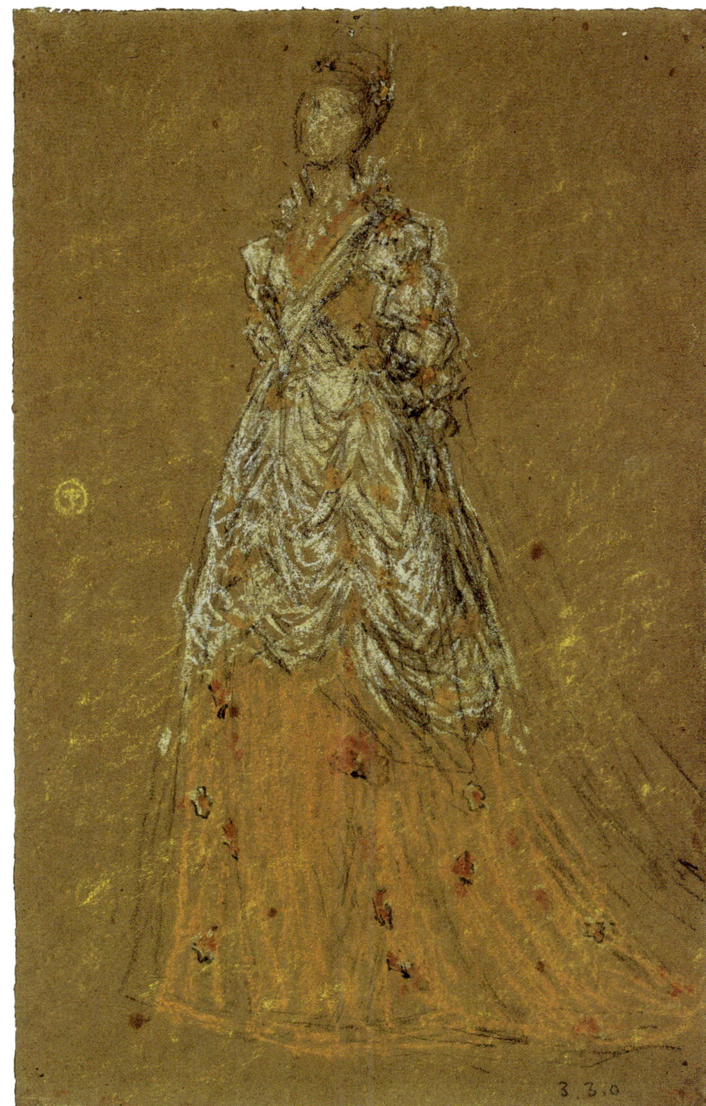

*Study for "Symphony in Flesh Color and Pink
(Mrs. Frederick R. Leyland)," 1871–74*
Pastel and charcoal on wove, brown paper
11¼ x 7¼ in. (28.5 x 18.4 cm)
Inscribed center left: [butterfly monogram]
Purchase with funds provided by the Council of
the Amon Carter Museum
1990.9

This study for the full-length portrait of Mrs. Frederick R. Leyland is an exquisite example of Whistler's meticulous preparation and mastery of aesthetic design. His training in Paris in 1856 stressed the importance of such studies, and Whistler executed at least ten known drawings for Mrs. Leyland's portrait. In this delicate costume study he leaves the sitter faceless, most likely because she did not pose for the work, and chooses instead to concentrate on the dress, with its elaborate chiffon sleeves and draped skirt adorned with orange rosettes. Working on brown, textured paper, he first drew the figure's silhouette in charcoal, then lightly applied an intricate network of shimmering orange, white, and yellow pastels. With these wisps of color and elegant lines, an aristocratic woman materializes, her hands clasped casually behind her back.

For the painting, *Symphony in Flesh Color and Pink: Portrait of Mrs. Frederick R. Leyland* (The Frick Collection, New York), Whistler used a pink palette, instead of orange, and presents Mrs. Leyland from behind so that her clasped hands are visible. Such an informal pose suggests the artist's close relationship with his subject, the wife of a wealthy Liverpool shipbuilder. Whistler remained an expatriate his entire adult life, residing primarily in England. He was a perennial guest at the Leyland's home, Speke Hall, and it was rumored that he and Mrs. Leyland were in love.

Regarded as one of the most influential proponents of the nineteenth-century's aesthetic movement, which celebrated "art for art's sake," Whistler regarded the purely visual aspects of a work as more important than its subject or narrative. To emphasize these aesthetic concerns Whistler assigned musical titles, such as "harmony," "arrangement," and "symphony," to his paintings. He also introduced oriental porcelain, rugs, fans, and other beautiful objects— selected from his own extensive collection of Japanese art—into his compositions. These art forms may well have inspired Whistler's creation of the distinctive butterfly symbol, which served as his signature on works created after 1869. In this drawing, the butterfly is visible in yellow pastel to the left of the subject, carefully balancing the subtle color, pattern, and line.

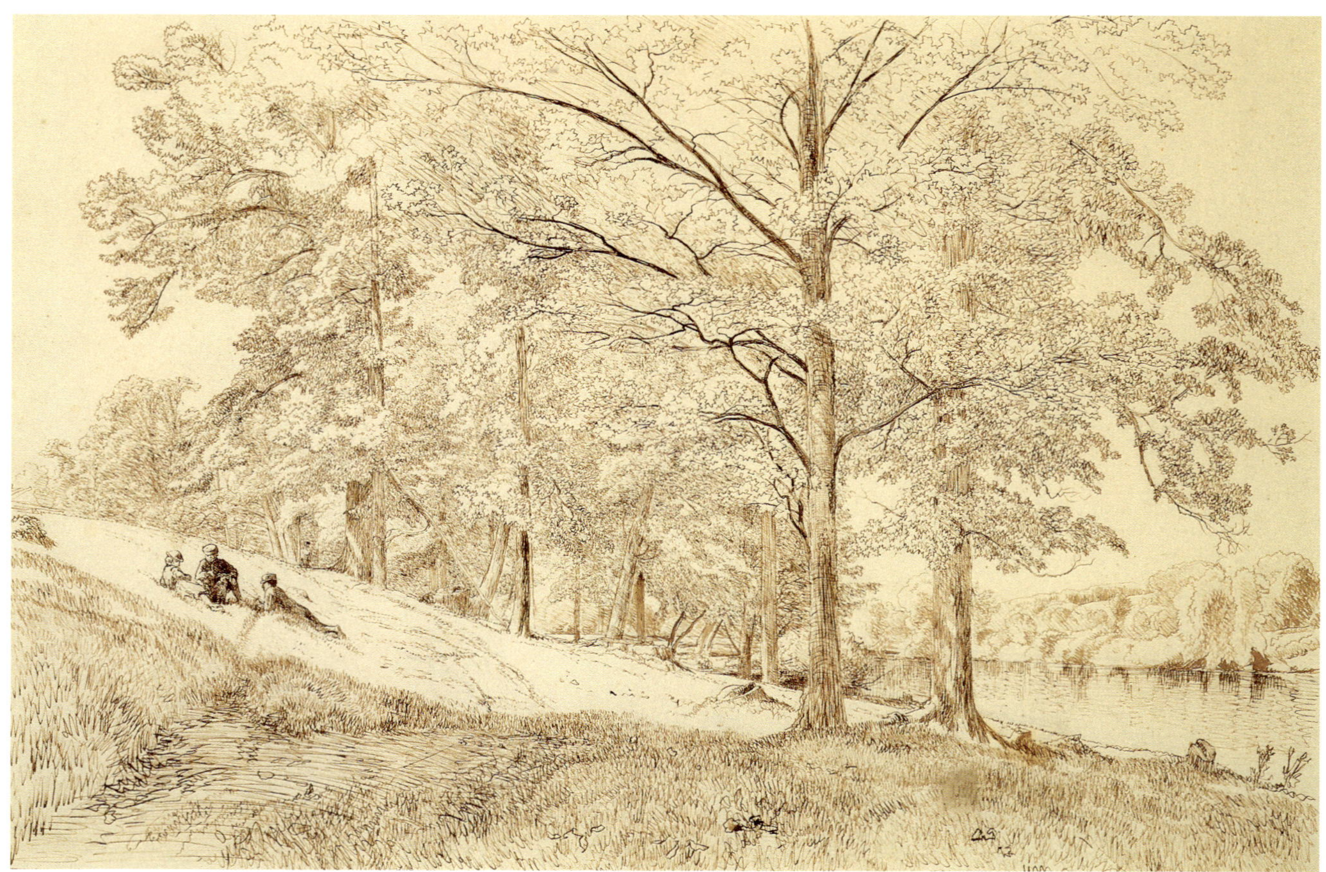

Aaron Draper Shattuck (1832–1928)

Farmington River, Connecticut, ca. 1865–75
Brown ink over graphite underdrawing on wove, buff paper
11⅞ x 17¾ in. (30.2 x 45.1 cm)
Inscribed lower left: *Farmington River—*
1983.1

Originally trained as a portrait painter, Aaron Draper Shattuck gravitated toward landscape painting while a student at the National Academy of Design in New York. There, he joined a spirited group of the genre's leading practitioners, including Jasper Cropsey, John Frederick Kensett, and Sanford Gifford. Shattuck began exhibiting his views of American scenery at the National Academy in 1855 and continued to show his work actively for over thirty years along the Northeastern seaboard, an area that provided him with ample subjects.

By mid-career the artist had come to prefer the tranquil, rural New England landscape to more spectacular scenery and drew praise for his evocation of commonplace, yet identifiable, locales, such as that portrayed in *Farmington River, Connecticut*. Made near the country retreat he began renting in 1866, this image celebrated Shattuck's affinity for expressive line at a time when drawings were increasingly looked upon as independent works of art and valued for the inti-

macy of their artistic expression. Shattuck filled his sheet with a network of tiny, animated lines, creating an anthology of varied, suggestive patterns: the oak leaves are defined by angular contours, the uneven bark by delicate, parallel striations, and the grass by brisk strokes that emulate its yielding textures. A bravura orchestration on a small scale, the drawing evokes the profusion of the natural world without reliance on the precise delineation of individual elements. A bright meadow in the middle ground, defined by the exposed sheet itself, supports three languorous, barefoot lads engaged in idle conversation, a popular literary and artistic motif of the period reflecting a nostalgic view of rural America.

In 1870 Shattuck left his New York studio and moved his family permanently to a farm near Granby, Connecticut. Although he stopped painting altogether in 1888, partially due to ill health, he lived well into the twentieth century, overseeing his farm, making violins, and successfully marketing his patented metal key for stretching canvases.

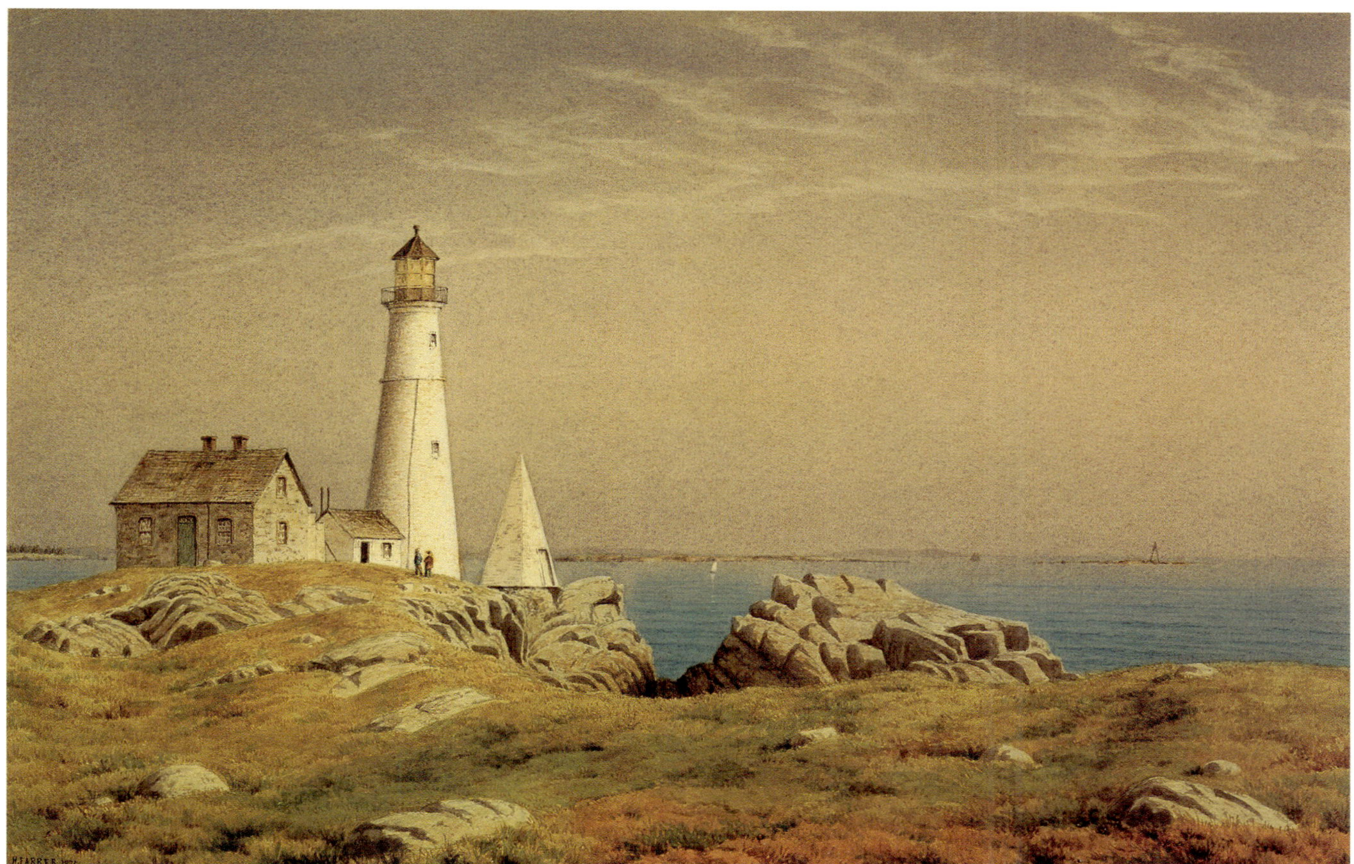

Henry Farrer (1843–1903)

Portland Head Light, Maine, 1875
Watercolor over graphite underdrawing on wove, cream paper
11⅞ x 18⅝ in. (30.2 x 47.3 cm)
Signed and dated lower left: *H. Farrer. 1875*
1990.11

Henry Farrer enjoyed a modest career creating small-scale, watercolor landscapes that were popular during the third quarter of the nineteenth century. These highly refined works depict quiet scenes full of the beauty and poetry the artist found in the American landscape. Arriving from London as a teenager, Farrer settled in New York City, where he joined a growing circle of avid watercolorists and became a founding member of the American Society of Painters in Water Color in 1866.

Portland Head Light, Maine—one in a series of coastal subjects made during a trip to the state in the summer of 1875 and singled out in the New York press when they were exhibited the following year—reflects the profound influence of English critic John Ruskin. The watercolor's unremittingly deliberate technique reflects Farrer's effort to accurately capture the scene. Farrer chose a placid vantage point, focusing on an equitable balance of land, sea, and sky, rather than the jagged rocks and roiling surf that lie at the foot of the eighteenth-century structure. The lighthouse and keeper's cottage located on Cape Elizabeth near the city of Portland, are signs of man's peaceful coexistence with nature. The pyramidal structure, added in 1870, contained an automatic, weight-powered machine that regularly struck a bell notifying ships that they were coming close to land. Farrer's understated technique indicates Ruskin's counsel to minimize the expression of individual brushstrokes. The white of the paper delicately interplays with the subtle application of watercolor, dictating the forms of the rocks, buildings, and sky, as well as the sail of the miniscule boat that appears near the horizon line in the center of the composition. Such watercolors became exceedingly popular as independent creative expressions on a par with oil paintings. Farrer's preference for the intimacy of works on paper led to his productive career as an etcher. In 1880 he translated this work into a print, later published in *Poets and Etchers* (1882). Indeed, printmaking gradually supplanted his keen interest in watercolor, and, in 1881, he became director of the New York Etching Club, of which he was a founder.

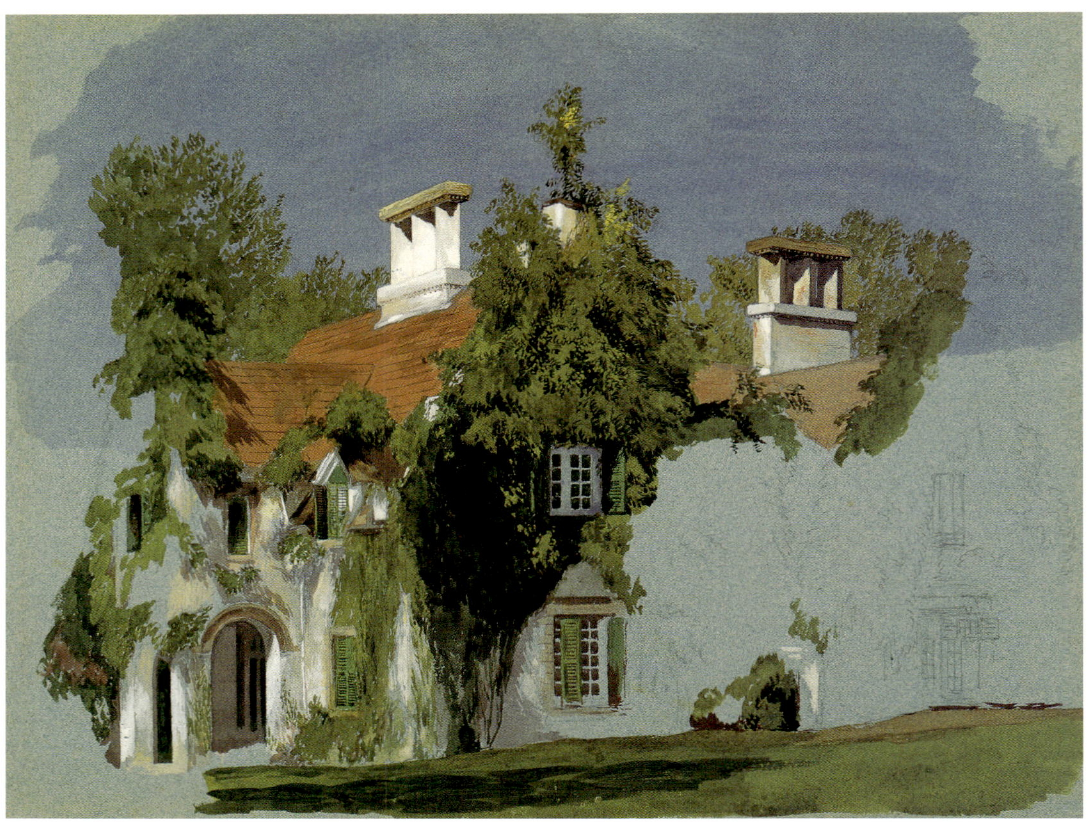

John Henry Hill (1839–1922)

"Sunnyside," Tarrytown, New York, ca. 1878
Transparent and opaque watercolor and graphite on wove, blue paper
12 x 16 in. (30.5 x 40.7 cm)
1981.38

During much of the nineteenth century, Americans regarded Sunnyside, Washington Irving's home on the Hudson River, as synonymous with the beloved author himself, who died in 1859. The public revered Irving, who had spent almost half of his adult life in Europe, for his popular stories that drew international attention to America's literary potential. The quaint Tarrytown homestead he purchased in 1835 seemed to embody the great writer's celebrated attributes of charm, whimsy, and modesty. Surrounded by his extended family, Irving spent the final thirteen years of his life at Sunnyside, receiving a constant flow of fledgling writers and distinguished admirers, whose accolades reflected those of a fond and grateful nation.

As an aspiring artist growing up across the Hudson in Nyack, New York, John Henry Hill began recording Sunnyside as early as 1857. By the 1870s, when Hill made this watercolor study, new literary movements had overtaken Irving's once singular prominence, yet the house remained a shrine to Irving's legend. Despite Hill's long familiarity with this architecturally outmoded Dutch farmhouse, he saw it anew, enlivening the structure through the luminous interplay of the brilliant green foliage of the trees and ivy that encircle its stepped gables with the flickering deep purple and blue shadows. This unfinished study reveals the artist's method of transforming a few loosely sketched graphite marks—still visible on the part of the sheet that remains unfinished—into a fully realized image of gleaming sunlight bouncing off the house's red shingles and white stone walls.

This intensely observed, firsthand sketch is a study for a finished and more measured watercolor, *Sunnyside with Picnickers* (Sleepy Hollow Restorations, Tarrytown, New York), of the type Hill actively exhibited in New York for over thirty years. In 1864 and 1878, he traveled to Europe where he furthered his study of English critic John Ruskin's precepts for the direct study of nature, first instilled by his father, artist John William Hill. The younger Hill also explored the American West with surveying expeditions in 1868 and 1870. Not long after executing *"Sunnyside,"* Hill returned to his family's farm in the Hudson River valley, where, like Irving, he would live for the remainder of his productive life.

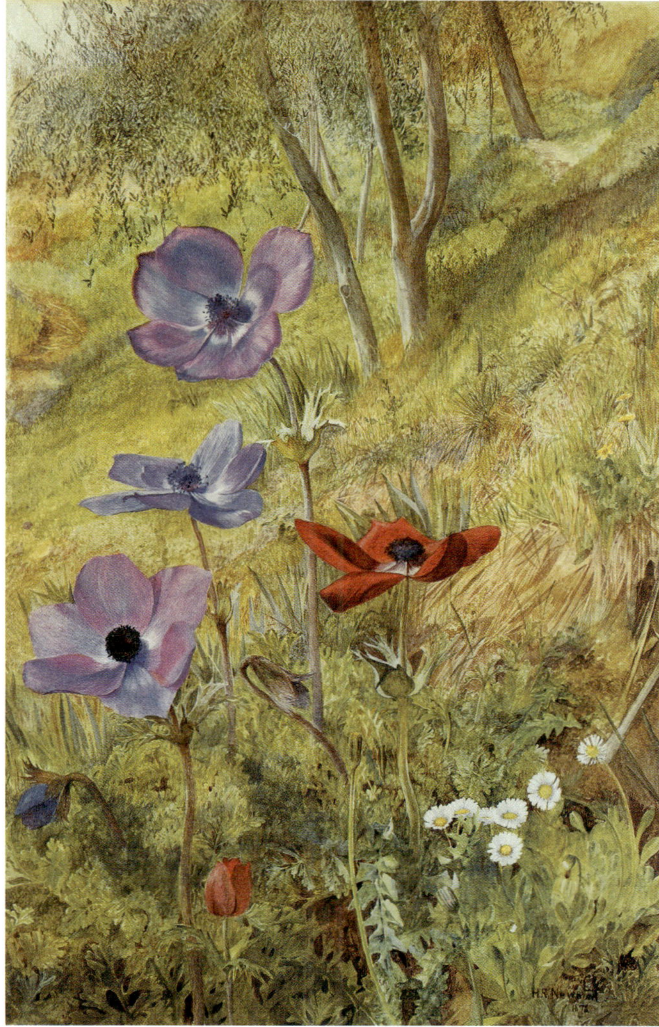

Henry Roderick Newman
(1843–1917)

Anemones, 1876
Watercolor on wove, off-white paper
18 x 11¾ in. (45.7 x 29.8 cm)
Signed and dated lower right: *H R Newman/1876*
Purchase with funds provided by Ruth Carter Stevenson
1985.281

When prosperous Americans and Englishmen visited Florence on the de rigueur cultural pilgrimage called the Grand Tour, they frequented the studios of the many expatriate American artists in residence there. Driven by ill health in 1870 from New York to the milder climate of Florence, Henry Roderick Newman, known for his precise flower studies and Venetian architectural views, found appreciative patrons among these English-speaking clients.

Like other young American artists of the 1860s, Newman had gravitated to the work of the American Pre-Raphaelites, an association of painters encouraged by the writings of John Ruskin to record the natural order, through its smallest nuance, in search of universal, divine truths. Newman, who had exhibited watercolors with the group in New York City, was a particularly avid devotee of Ruskin, whom he eventually met after relocating to Italy. The Englishman praised Newman's carefully conceived watercolors, providing approbation of momentous import for the artist. Adhering to a meticulous, high-keyed approach, Newman sustained the Pre-Raphaelite sensibility in his Italian work at the same time the style was being supplanted in America by the more painterly approach that characterized the last decades of the nineteenth century.

Newman's growth as a watercolorist continued to be monitored by American periodicals in their coverage of expatriate artists working in Florence, and his flower studies, like *Anemones*, were singled out for their immense power and luminosity. Newman achieved a vivid, overall brightness by employing jewel-like colors and allowing bits of bare white paper to appear through the dense leaves and grasses. Shown here in various states of growth, *Anemone coronaro*, a spring wild flower that thrives in the Tuscan climate, bears delicate petals, ranging in color from red to purple, that were rendered by Newman in precise, deftly blended strokes. The informal, uncultivated outdoor setting belies the artist's careful calculations underlying an image that offers the unexpected pleasure of encountering at eye level wild flowers growing on an Italian hillside.

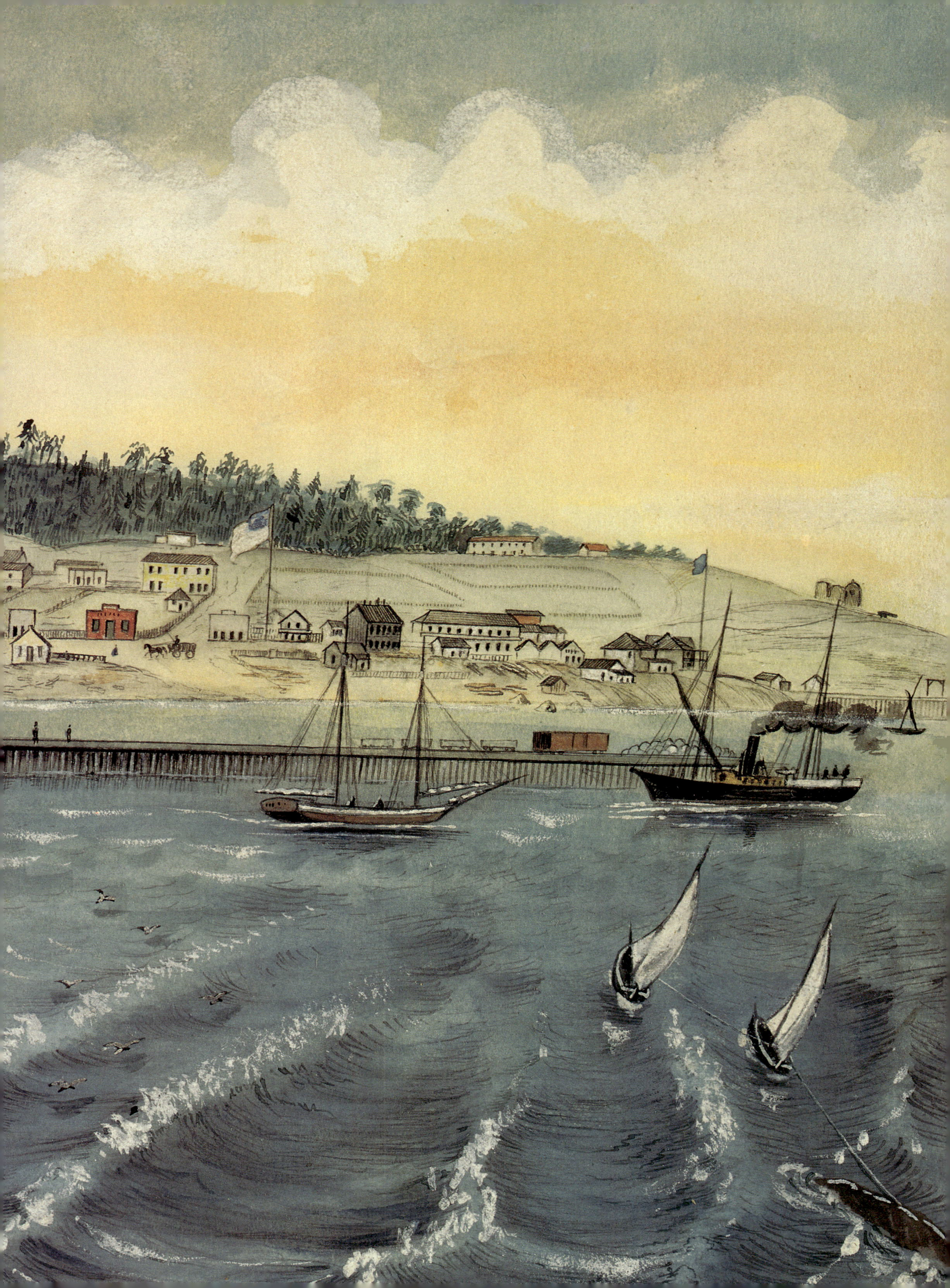

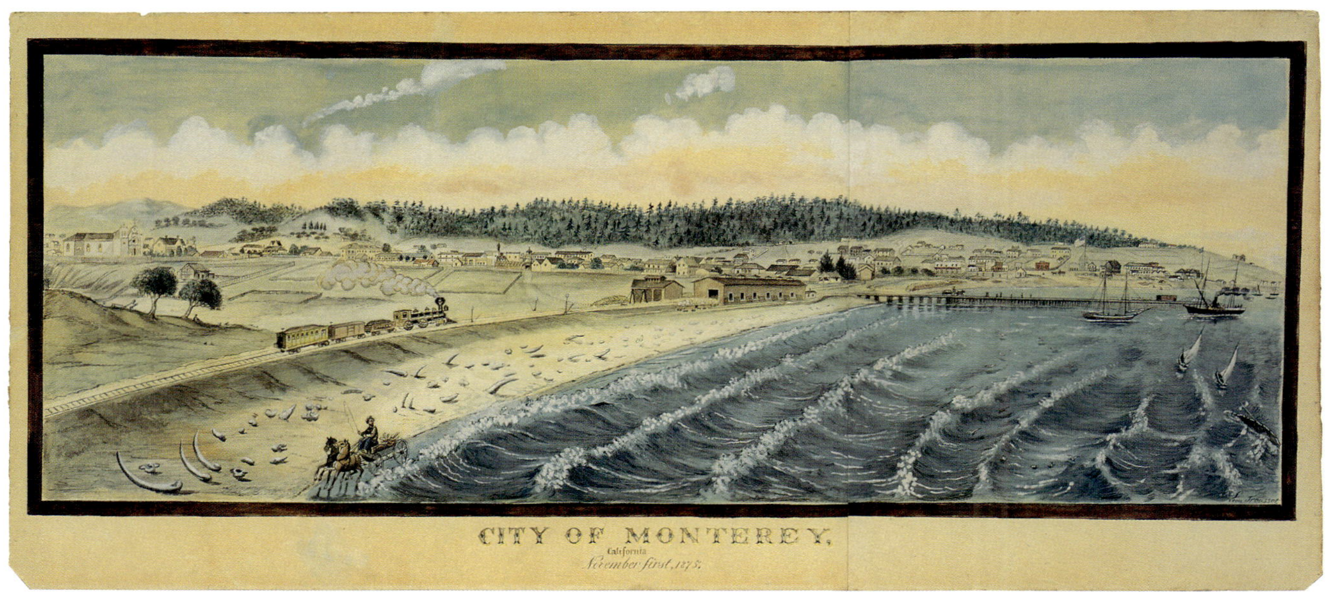

Leon Trousset (active ca. 1870–ca. 1900)

City of Monterey, California. November First, 1875, 1875
Transparent and opaque watercolor and ink on joined, wove, buff paper
20⅛ x 45¹⁵⁄₁₆ in. (51.1 x 114.5 cm)
Signed, dated, and inscribed, lower center: *CITY OF MONTEREY,*
California. November first, 1875.; lower right: *Leon Trousset*
1977.1

Sweeping visual panoramas in the form of prints, drawings, and photographs symbolized the economic aspirations of many evolving communities in the American West. In 1875 Leon Trousset painted an expansive view of Monterey, California, a community eager to promote its commercial potential just six years after the transcontinental railroad opened the West to immigration and trade. The watercolor's extraordinary detail includes the chapel of the old Presidio, built in 1770, evidence of the town's roots as a Spanish settlement. The whaling industry in Monterey continued to thrive throughout much of the nineteenth century; Trousset took delight in the decorative placement of the whalebone shards that evidently littered the shore. A narrative vignette to the right depicts two sailboats towing a whale carcass to the wharf's rendering plant, where oil was extracted from the blubber.

In addition to the area's natural harbor, salubrious climate, scenic beauty, and rich agricultural potential, leading citizens placed considerable faith in the new Monterey & Salinas Valley Railroad as another catalyst to growing prosperity. Created with financial backing from the area's farmers, the narrow-gauge, eighteen-and-one-half-mile track had opened the year before Trousset executed this view.

Shown approaching Monterey's storage depot, the train boasted a passenger car fabricated in Monterey and an engine made by the Baldwin Locomotive Works in Pennsylvania. The horse-drawn cart at the water's edge underscores the improvements wrought by this cheaper and quicker means of transporting crops to the port at Monterey.

The people of Monterey also embraced the fine arts as a community asset. For many years this watercolor hung in a Monterey bar and restaurant operated by Jules Simoneau, like Trousset a native of France. Simoneau, a generous patron of the arts, provided a meeting place for the local bohemians, who soon would turn the town into a cultural mecca for artists and writers, including Robert Louis Stevenson, who arrived in 1879. After railroad magnates opened the spectacular and luxurious Hotel Del Monte on Monterey Bay in 1880, the ensuing influx of wealthy Euro-Americans forever altered the character of this peaceful, self-sufficient community and its largely Mexican population.

The duration of Trousset's sojourn in California is unknown. Other works by the obscure artist depict settlements in Mexico, West Texas, and New Mexico.

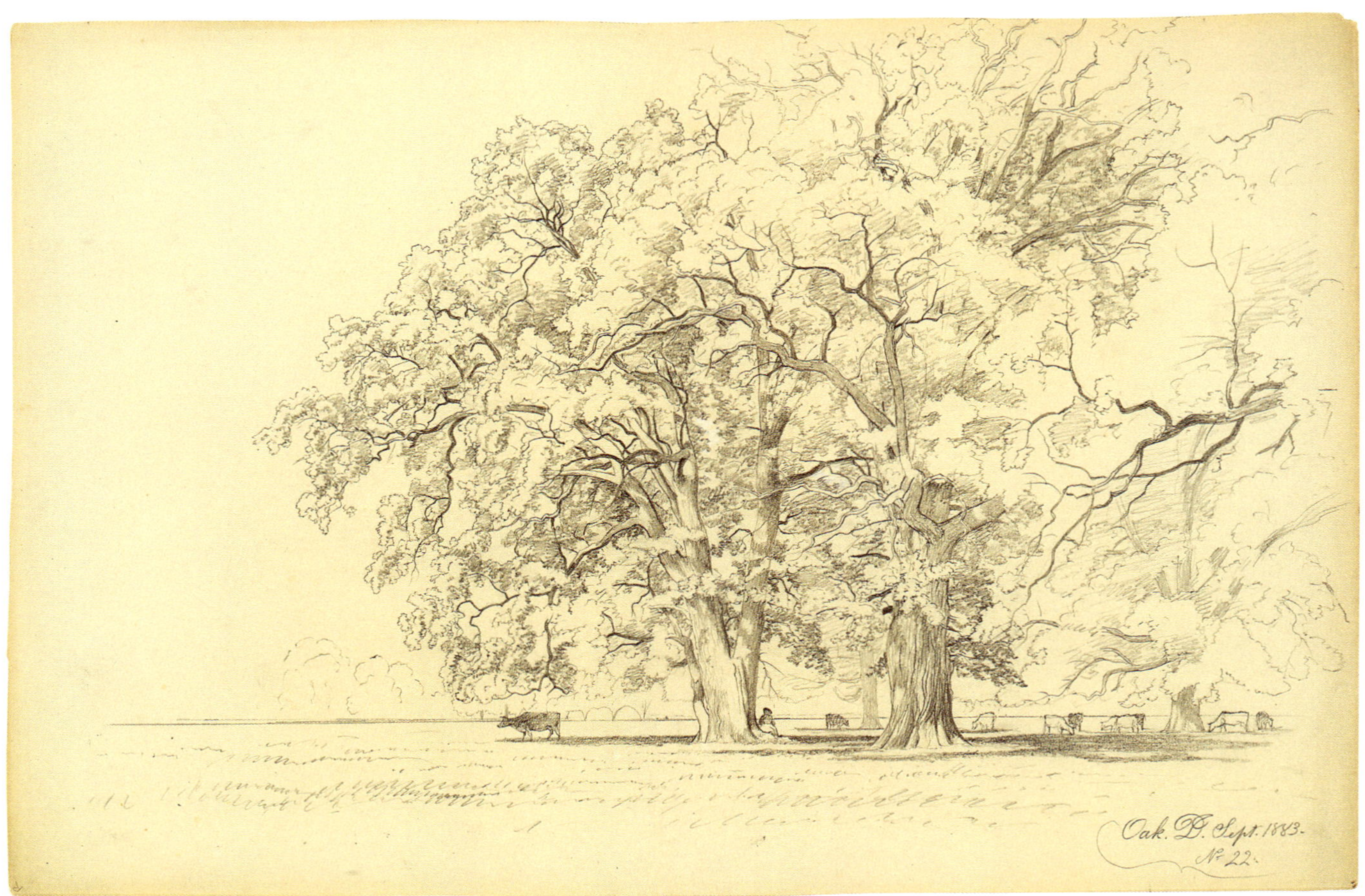

David Johnson (1827–1908)

Oak, 1883
Graphite and opaque white on wove, tan paper
12⅜ x 19 in. (31.4 x 48.2 cm)
Signed, dated, and inscribed lower right: *Oak. DJ.*
[monogram] *Sept. 1883./Nº 22.*
1983.151

Artists of the mid- to late-nineteenth century undertook a prolonged study of the American landscape through the most direct means available. This majestic, open stand of towering bur oaks induced artist David Johnson to sketch the scene on the spot. Essentially self-taught, although he also seems to have studied briefly with the highly regarded landscape painter Jasper F. Cropsey, Johnson was a member of a collegial circle of landscape painters based in New York City. The group, which included Johnson's famous friend John Frederick Kensett, advocated an artist's regular immersion in the countryside in pursuit of subject matter.

Johnson initially learned his craft by copying prints; his acute fidelity to nature in his mature work reflects this laborious and focused aspect of his training, as well as the contemporary taste for realism. During the 1880s Johnson's empirical fascination with nature led him to make countless tree drawings, which he carefully annotated with the month and year of execution, genus of the tree, and a reference number. Some drawings made during seasonal excursions, primarily into the scenic countryside of the Northeast, were studies for oils; others stood alone as captivating fragments of the American landscape.

Oak may depict a site in upstate New York, an area Johnson particularly favored. Combining an emphasis on contour, shading, and selective detail, the artist provided just enough visual information to impart the oaks' special characteristics. The trunks support a dark armature of limbs reinforced with graphite, while the tufts of foliage are more sketchily applied. The wiry, expressive branches, an interest in the effects of dappled light as it filters through the leaves, and the merging crowns of the four large trees massed together create a remarkably suggestive arboreal vignette, despite the lack of fully realized detail. Acting as a nurturing element within the broad natural universe, the wide-spreading limbs of the stately trees provide shade for grazing cattle and a solitary seated figure.

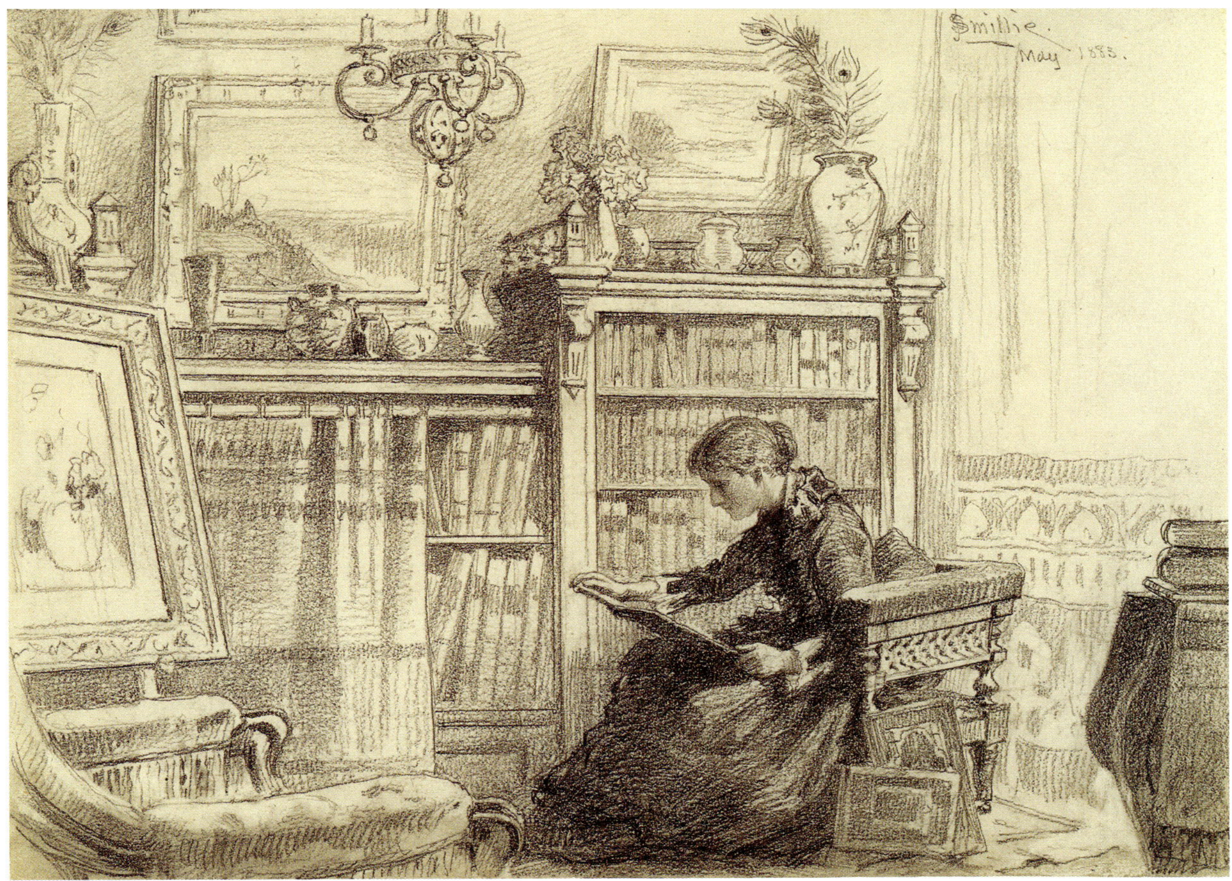

James David Smillie (1833–1909)

A Corner at Home, 1883
Graphite on wove, off-white paper mounted to board
10 x 14 in. (25.4 x 35.6 cm)
Signed and dated upper right: *J S* [monogram] *millie./May 1883.*
1982.34

The growth of the publishing industry during the nineteenth century necessitated a steady flow of original illustrations. In his diary entry for May 12, 1883, James David Smillie writes of making a graphite drawing depicting Annie, his wife of two years, in the parlor of their New York townhouse. After being translated to the etching medium, the image in the following year would illustrate Charles Lamb's essay "Detached Thoughts on Books and Reading" in a modern edition of his popular, semiautobiographical *Essays of Elia*, originally published in 1823.

Trained by his father, an artist also named James Smillie, the younger man was highly regarded for his technical skill as a printmaker and illustrator. Experience as a bank note engraver between 1862 and 1864 initially led him to undertake popular engravings after the paintings of the great masters, but Smillie's creative aspirations soon extended beyond the reproduction of paintings. He was a leading advocate for recognition of both drawing and etching as independent artistic expressions and helped found the New York Etching Club in 1877.

In *A Corner at Home*, Smillie employs soft pencil to capture each element of the ensemble of objects prescribed by contemporary taste. Packed bookcases, an array of ceramics, original paintings with decorative frames, and fine furnishings speak to the couple's comfort and prosperity. The valance drawn over the bookcase, the window drapery, and the fashionable peacock feathers further distinguish the highly textured interior. The artist anticipated the etched version of the drawing by emphasizing light and dark contrasts. He rendered Annie and the table at the right edge of the composition in darker tones, so they would stand out more emphatically when translated to print. Smillie left the paper bare in the passages where he wanted to indicate the brilliant sunlight illuminating the room.

The image of a woman bending intently over her book at home was a popular theme during this period; it signified a refined aesthetic taste and the desire for intellectual improvement. The domestic happiness in Smillie's scene was irrevocably shattered when Annie died suddenly of pneumonia in 1895 at the age of forty-nine.

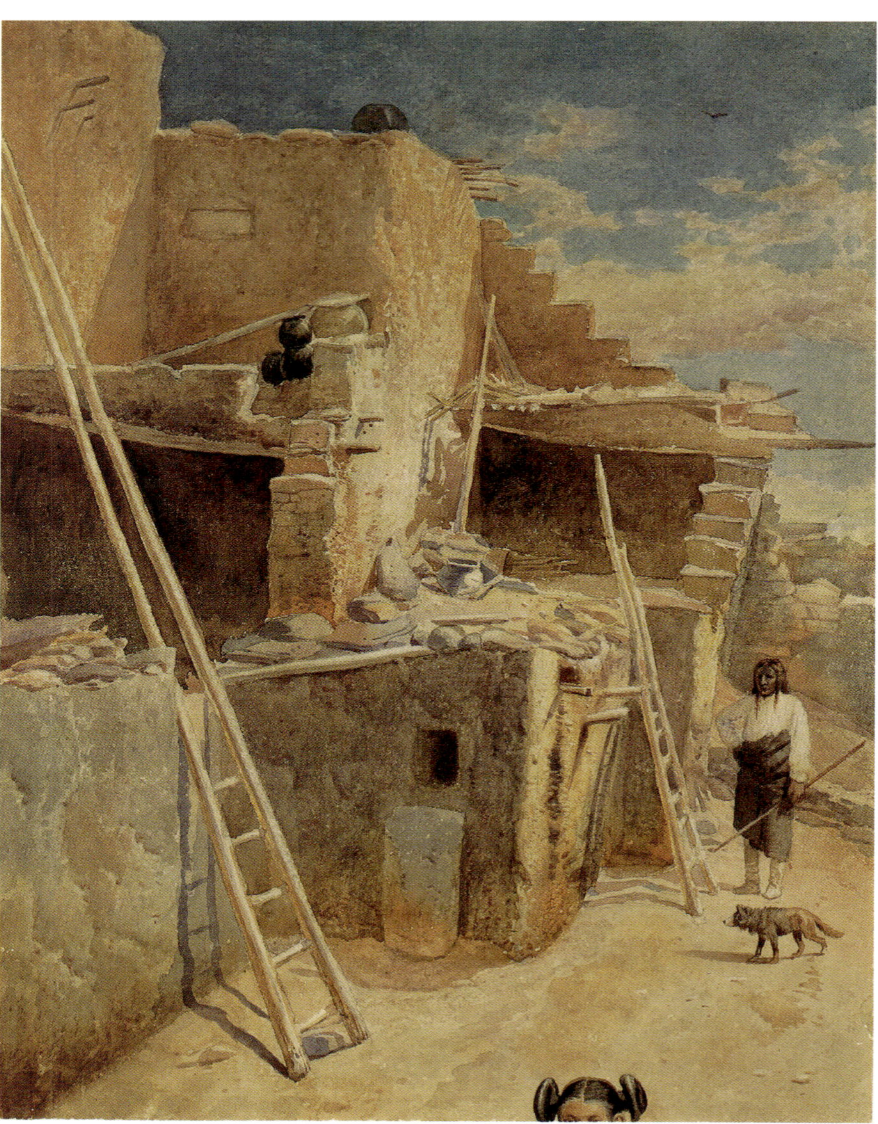

Peter Moran
(1841–1914)

Walpi, Arizona, 1881
Watercolor and graphite on laid, cream paper
17¼ x 13¾ in. (43.8 x 34.9 cm)
Signed, dated, and inscribed on paper fragment
trimmed from sheet: *Walpi./Arizona/P. Moran*
1965.81

Over the second half of the nineteenth century, exploration of the American West evolved increasingly toward careful ethnological documentation. During a sketching trip to New Mexico in the summer of 1881, Peter Moran joined U.S. Army Lieutenant John G. Bourke's expedition to the Hopi communities of northeastern Arizona, thereby becoming one of the first outsiders to witness the ancient rites of this highly structured and secretive tribe. The Hopis had lived relatively impervious to the outside world since Spanish incursions led them to relocate atop high desert mesas in the seventeenth century. Now, the adventurous Anglo population increasingly infringed upon their insular lifestyle.

Bourke and Moran made the arduous trip to the village of Walpi, located atop a 600-foot mesa, where, by convincing the reluctant Indians to permit access to their five underground ceremonial chambers or *kivas,* they likely became the first outsiders to witness the Hopi's sacred Snake Dance. Moran's watercolor sketch, however, records a more informal moment in the community's daily life. He portrays Walpi's conjoined pueblos, whose upper levels were accessible by ladders propped against the stone and clay walls, and the distinctively bulbous earthenware vessels that functioned as chimneys when stacked. Documenting the inhabitants, Moran portrays a man wearing the Hopi's traditional shirt and pants covered with a blanket wrap, along with one of the ubiquitous mongrel dogs commented upon by members of the expedition. In the foreground, the face of a female figure has been abruptly trimmed off the bottom of the sheet. Only her characteristic whorl hairstyle representing the squash blossom, a symbol of fertility worn by unmarried women, remains. The report generated by the Bourke expedition provided important anthropological information regarding the Hopi people, and in 1882 Walpi was included in the Hopi Indian Reservation set aside by President Chester A. Arthur.

The Bourke expedition was one of several that took Moran to the West. He had learned to paint from his older brothers, Edward and Thomas, and later taught at the Philadelphia School of Design for Women. While his work in the field is historically very important, Moran became most famous in his lifetime for his etchings, some of which he based on his western experiences.

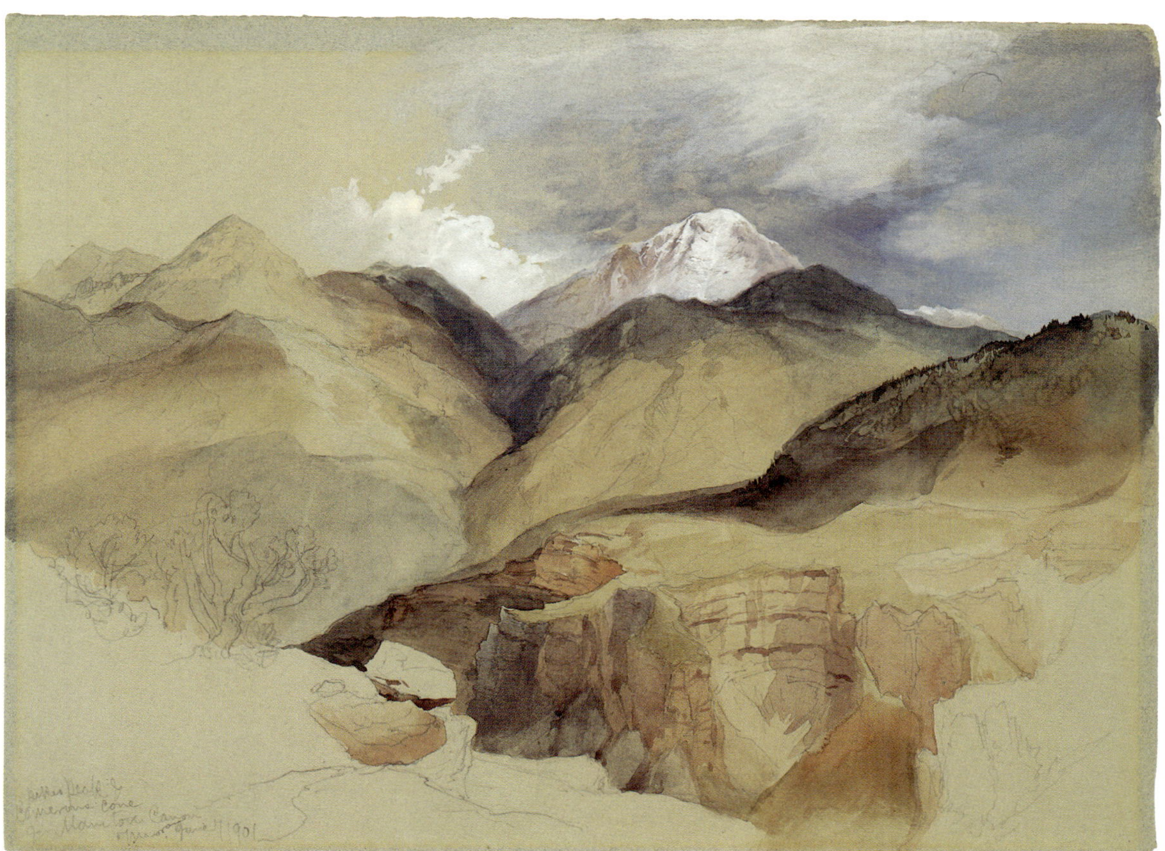

Thomas Moran (1837–1926)

Pikes Peak, Cameron Cone, and Manitou Cañon, 1901
Transparent and opaque watercolor and graphite on wove, faded blue paper
10⅞ x 15⅛ in. (27.6 x 38.4 cm)
Signed, dated, and inscribed lower left: *Pikes Peak &/Camerons* [sic]
Cone/& Manitou Canon [sic]/*TMoran June 7 1901*
1973.66

Thomas Moran's visual interpretations of the West's most magnificent scenery helped shape America's vision of the region's splendors. Among the most prominent of the many images created by nineteenth-century artists and photographers, Moran's works played a central role in the creation of the National Park system and abetted the rise of western commerce and tourism. The artist's long life span ensured that he would witness the advances in modern civilization that his artistic contributions helped stimulate.

In 1901 Moran traveled through Colorado, retracing his steps of nearly thirty years earlier. This work numbers among hundreds of field sketches, some enhanced with passages of watercolor, that Moran rendered onsite as raw source material for his oil paintings. This drawing indicates that the passing of years did not dim the artist's fresh, direct response to nature's icons. A graphite sketch and translucent layers of watercolor washes afford a spatial framework for the drawing's pictorial climax: the stunning, isolated peak carefully modeled with white opaque watercolor.

Facing west from the vicintiy of Colorado Springs, Moran depicted Cameron Cone to the south of Pikes Peak and, beneath his feet, the deep canyons supporting the burgeoning communities that had erupted along the Front Range of the Rocky Mountains. By the time of Moran's first visit to the area during the 1870s, developers had already begun to entice wealthy Americans to the salubrious climate and beautiful scenery. Once a symbol of the frenzy surrounding the gold rush, Pikes Peak now stood as a beacon for the fine resorts that rose beside natural mineral springs. Moran, who had important patrons in the area, readily availed himself of modern advances in lodging and transportation. The day he made the drawing of Pikes Peak, he also sketched from the cog railway, then considered the most advanced of modern transports, which had operated from Manitou Springs to the summit of Pikes Peak since 1891. Making the 1901 trip under contract to the Santa Fe Railroad, the artist, now in his sixties, created images that were used by commercial interests to promote the region as a tourist destination. Moran thus adapted to the exigencies brought about by this rapidly growing region, the settlement of which ran parallel to the career of an artist whose passion for the West never waned.

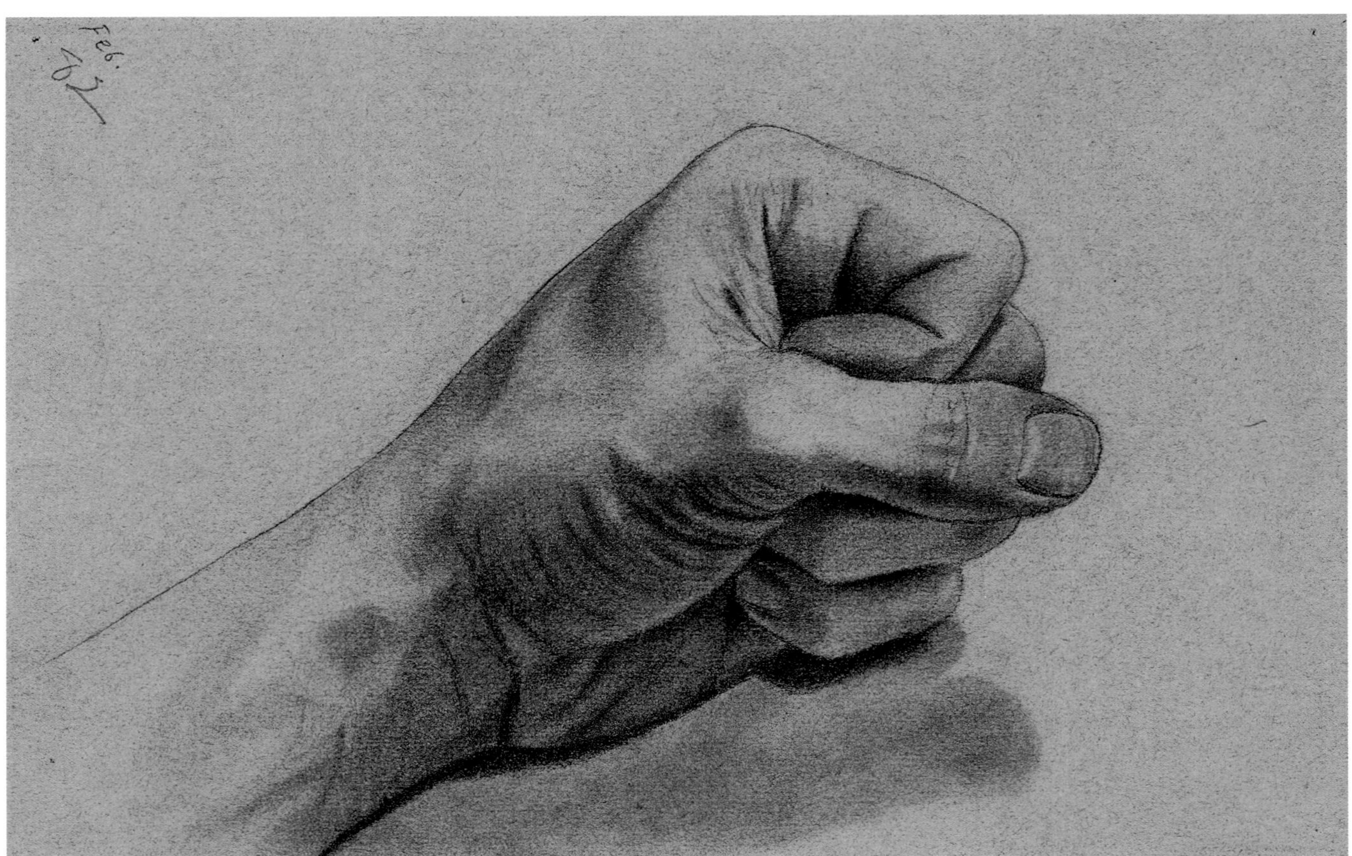

John Haberle (1856–1933)

Haberle's Left Hand, 1882
Graphite on laid, blue paper
6 x 9½ in. (15.2 x 24.1 cm)
Dated, upper left: *Feb./82;* on reverse, upper left: *Feb. 7th 82*
1985.286

John Haberle built his artistic career by blurring reality and artifice. So lifelike were his famed still-life paintings—meticulous renderings of paper money, stamps, and newspaper clippings—that both critics and collectors accused him of gluing actual objects to the canvas. Like other contemporary trompe l'oeil painters, such as John Frederick Peto and William M. Harnett, Haberle succeeded in this visual deception by rendering commonplace objects true to their actual size and color, employing meticulous, nearly imperceptible, brushwork. This accomplished graphite drawing of Haberle's left hand, dating just prior to his career as a still-life painter, represents a keen interest in heightened realism and accurate draftsmanship that would soon inform the artist's work in oil.

Haberle grew up in New Haven, Connecticut, where his parents encouraged his youthful fascination with drawing, permitting him at age fourteen to apprentice with a printing firm. During the early 1880s, while still in his twenties, Haberle joined the large staff of field collectors, technicians, and mechanical draftsmen employed by Othniel Charles Marsh, Yale University's famed paleontologist, who was at this time producing some of his most important publications on extinct species. Evidence suggests that Haberle continued to refine his skills as a draftsman in Marsh's laboratory, making illustrations of the dinosaur fossils the scientist had gathered on expeditions to the American West. As this highly naturalistic drawing from the period illustrates, such training enhanced Haberle's understanding of the internal structure of anatomical forms. Formal art instruction in the nineteenth century centered on the human figure; yet, lacking funds for art school, Haberle relied on his arm, hands, and feet as models. Using blue paper as his support, Haberle brought a sense of weight and grace to his clenched fist, carefully noting the effect of this gesture on muscle and skin. Adding a slight shadow beneath the solitary form, he provided a further sense of spatial reality.

By 1884 Haberle had secured the financial means to study for a year at the National Academy of Design in New York. Afterward, he returned to New Haven and found success marketing his diminutive trompe l'oeil paintings to middle-class businessmen.

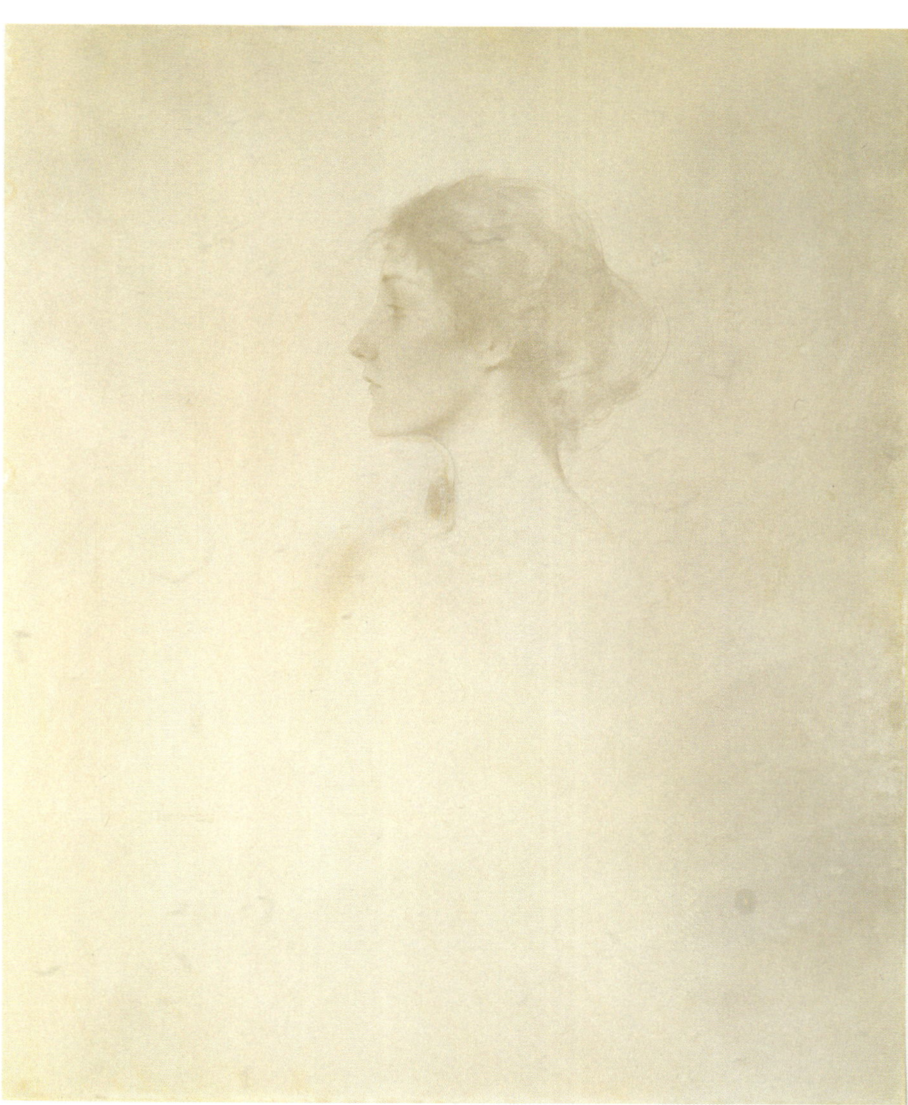

Thomas Wilmer Dewing
(1851–1938)

Portrait of a Woman, ca. 1894
Silverpoint on prepared paper
25 x 21¼ in. (63.5 x 54.0 cm)
Signed lower left: *T W Dewing*
1986.61

A widespread appreciation of drawing as an independent art form, coupled with an admiration for the aesthetics of the Italian Renaissance, contributed to Thomas Dewing's fascination with the profile portrait and the silverpoint technique during the 1890s. Over a long career of paying homage to beautiful young women through countless oils and pastels, Dewing executed only a handful of delicate silverpoints, an exacting process that involved drawing on prepared paper with a metal stylus.

In this drawing, the largest of his known silverpoints, Dewing captures both the incisive and ethereal qualities of his subject (most likely Julia [Dudie] Baird), one of the accomplished women who served as models for the artist's intimate circle of painters and sculptors. Dewing's mastery of silverpoint is evident in the dense buildup of linear marks that create discreet areas of shadow and the single, unwavering line that describes the contour of the subject's refined features. Her tousled hair, gently modeled cheekbones, and graceful bearing are all enhanced by the tarnished metal's warm tonalities.

This profile format, a classical type of portraiture adopted by fifteenth-century Italian painters, enabled Dewing to marry the image of the fashionable modern women he so admired with the art tradition of the High Renaissance. This aesthetic permeated Dewing's circle, which included artist and architect Charles Adams Platt, to whom Dewing gave this drawing around the time of Platt's 1893 marriage to his second wife, Eleanor Hardy Bunker, the widow of artist Dennis Miller Bunker.

Dewing and Platt were neighbors in Cornish, New Hampshire, where Dewing summered during the late 1880s and 1890s. This small community provided a pastoral setting for an elite group of New York City architects and artists, such as sculptor Augustus Saint-Gaudens, who produced dignified, yet naturalistic, profile portraits in bronze relief. Saint-Gaudens, Dewing, and Platt figured prominently among this group of stylish aesthetes, united by their mutual interest in reviving the eternal ideals they found inherent in classical prototypes.

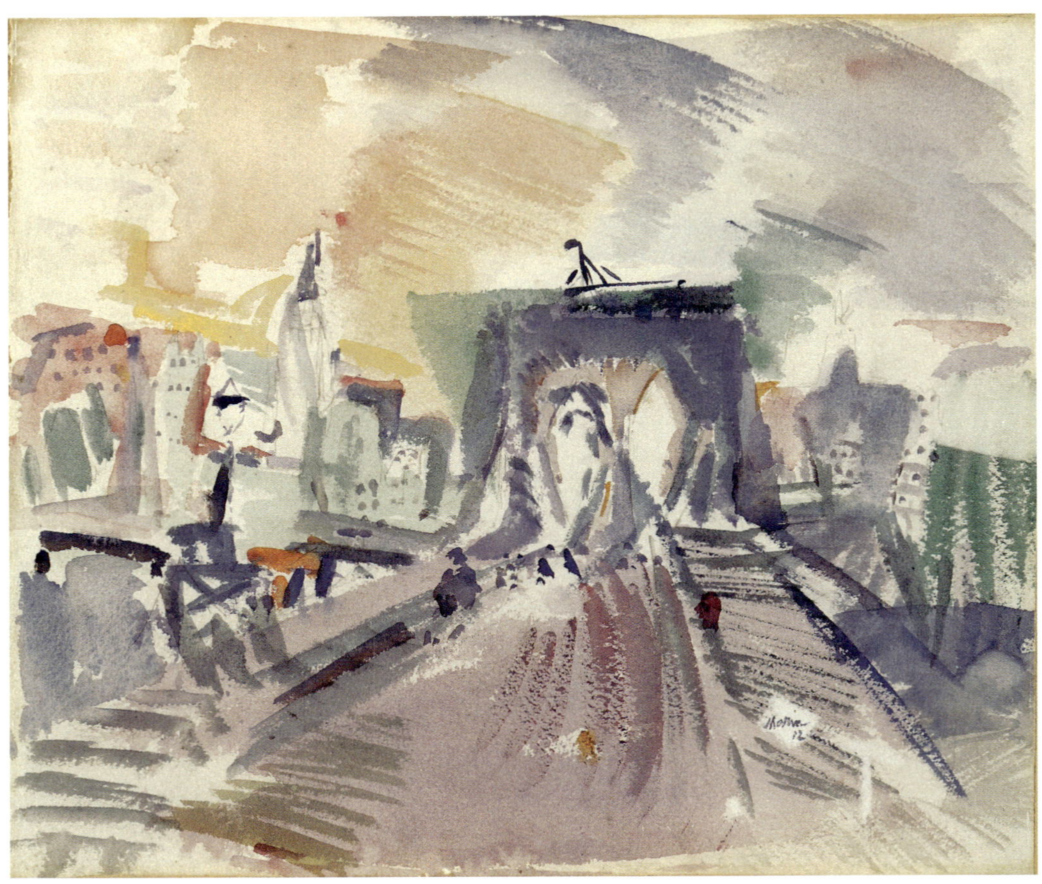

John Marin (1870–1953)

Brooklyn Bridge, 1912
Watercolor and graphite on wove, off-white paper
13¾ x 16⅝ in. (34.9 x 42.2 cm)
Signed and dated lower right: *Marin/12*
Purchase with funds from the Ruth Carter Stevenson Acquisitions Endowment, In honor of Sherman E. Lee, Trustee, Amon Carter Museum, 1972–present
1998.142

Brooklyn Bridge belongs to a small group of watercolors that heralded John Marin as one of the most talented and radical avant-garde artists of his era. Marin featured this work along with other watercolors of New York City in his ground-breaking January 1913 exhibition, *Watercolors and Oils by John Marin,* at Alfred Stieglitz's Little Galleries of the Photo-Secession (known as 291 for its address on Fifth Avenue). Exhibited for an entire month before the Armory Show introduced modern art to a broad American audience, the works were auspicious in their formal audacity.

Marin had returned to New York City in 1910 following several extended trips to Europe. He marveled at the city's rapid transformation into the economic center of the twentieth century and began recording the personal sensations that the energized metropolis produced. Although created during the Victorian era and completed in 1883, the Brooklyn Bridge emerged in Marin's work as a potent symbol of American technological ingenuity and, thereafter, became a common modernist motif for both writers and artists.

Exploiting watercolor's capacity for spontaneity, Marin combined a lively patchwork of pale, pastel washes and vigorous brushstrokes to denote an urban environment so frenetic that even the sky echoes a sense of urgency. Detail is blurred in this undulating cityscape. The bridge, seen from the Brooklyn side, serves as the composition's central focus; by extending it into the foreground, Marin sweeps the viewer toward Manhattan's emerging skyscrapers and the figures, denoted by dark patches of blue, who traverse the pedestrian walkway. To the left of the bridge, Marin placed the towering Woolworth Building, which, upon its completion in 1913, would reign for a while as the tallest building in the world. Marin's passion for watercolor, with its capacity for immediacy and freedom of expression, remained a cornerstone for the artist's new initiatives throughout his long career.

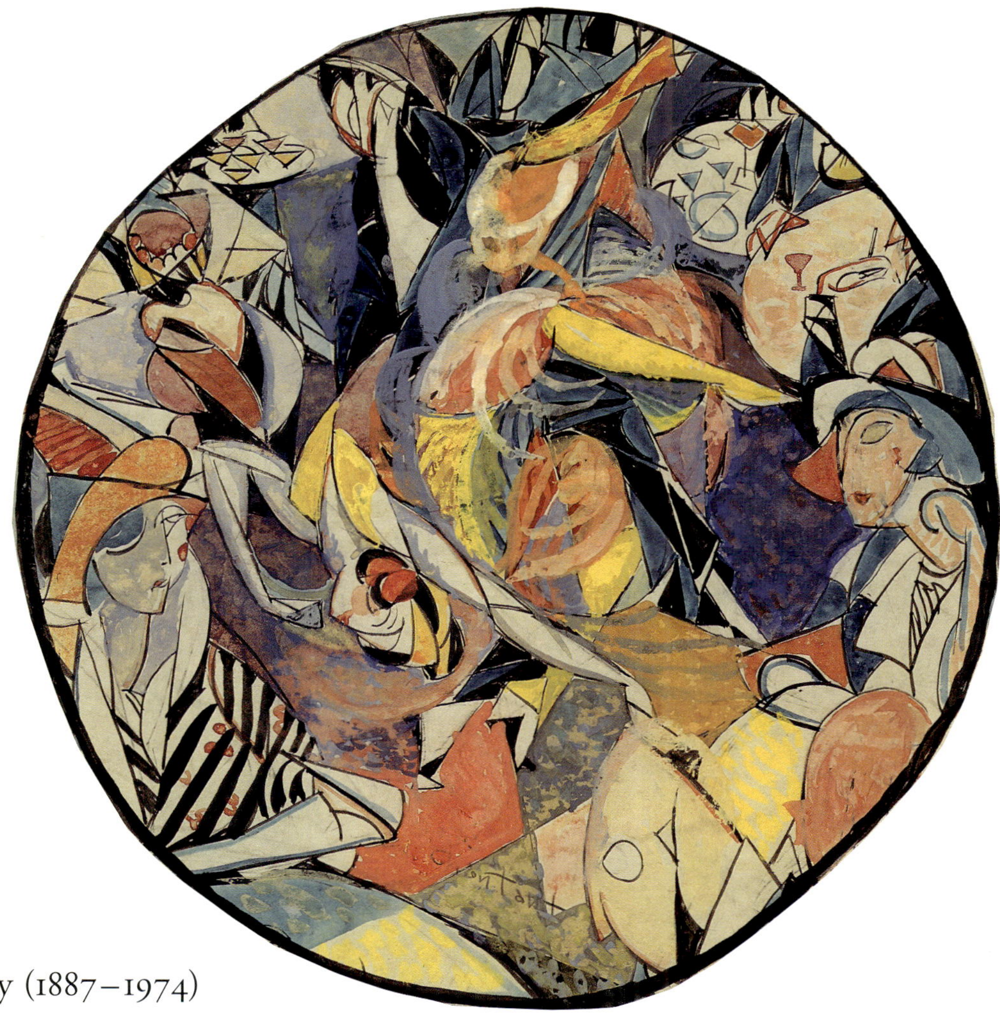

James Henry Daugherty (1887–1974)

Cabaret (Café Chantant), 1914
Ink, transparent and opaque watercolor, and graphite on wove, cream paper
12⅛ in. dia. (30.8 cm)
Signed, dated, and inscribed, lower center in image: *Chantant*; on reverse, center right: *Cabaret/JD/1914*
1984.18

In 1914 and 1915, a series of lively color abstractions, depicting aspects of modern American life, graced the cover of the New York *Herald* Sunday magazine section. James Daugherty's watercolor illustrations reflected his contact with the avant-garde that in 1913 had taken New York by storm at the Armory Show, the city's first major exhibition of modern American and European art. Daugherty's initial foray into modernism embraced the radical restructuring of form that characterized such art, and like his friend Joseph Stella, Daugherty employed exaggerated form and expressive color to conjure up the spirited, even hedonistic, revelry of modern life.

In *Cabaret* Daugherty scrambled the figures of stylishly attired men and women into prismatic fragments as if seen through a kaleidoscope, an association reinforced by the drawing's circular format. This vortex, however bewildering, accurately describes the intimacy between performer and audience that defined the café style, a recent Parisian import, where theater-type seating gave way to patrons at tables sharing the same floor as the entertainment. Daugherty's dancer contorts her body in an improbably deep backward bend while being watched by patrons arranged around the edges of the sheet.

The work relates closely to one of several drawings reproduced in the *Herald* (January 15, 1915) under the heading "Broadway Nights," Daugherty's renderings of New York's fashionable set. Captions like *Dynamism of a Bar Keeper Mixing a Drink* assume a readership attuned to an often satirical response to the avant-garde. The phrase references the work of the Italian futurists, whose "dynamism" Daugherty emulated by employing the concept of simultaneity or the concurrent experience of different senses. Daugherty's ability to draw on a popular vein of American culture continued after World War I, when he began to work in a more representational, figurative style as a muralist and illustrator of children's books.

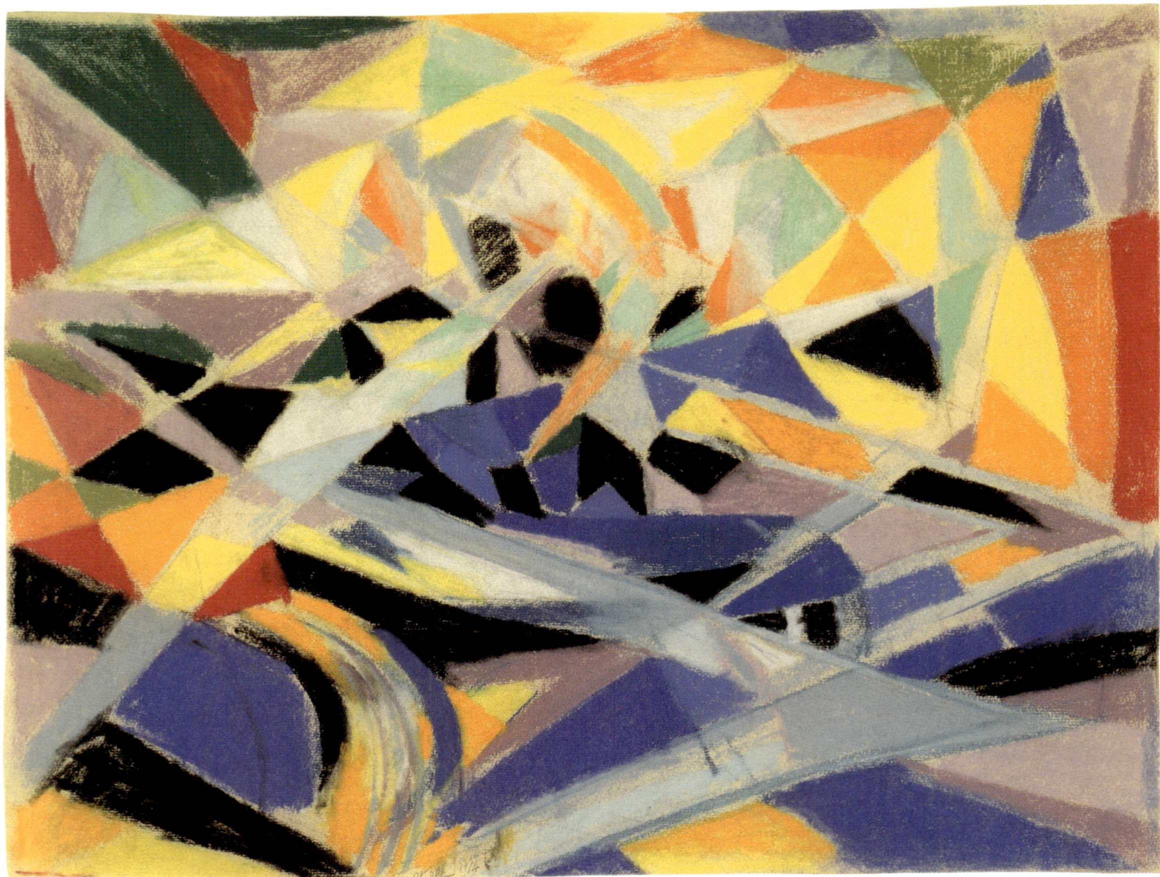

Joseph Stella (1877–1946)

Futurist Composition, 1914
Pastel over graphite on laid, cream paper
16³⁄₈ x 21⁷⁄₈ in. (41.6 x 55.5 cm)
Purchase with funds provided by the Council of the Amon Carter Museum
Signed and dated lower center: [Ste]*lla 1914*
1995.15

Joseph Stella began incorporating the modernist idiom in his work after a serendipitous experience at Coney Island led to an artistic breakthrough for the thirty-six-year-old painter. Emigrating from Italy to the United States as a teenager, Stella had attracted modest critical success with his exquisite figure drawings and atmospheric industrial scenes in charcoal. Even so, Stella felt alienated in his adopted country, and in 1909 he returned to Europe for four years.

When Stella returned to the United States, he found himself unexpectedly invigorated by the country's prominence in the development of new technologies. An encounter with the dazzling electric lights of Coney Island in the fall of 1913 led to the stunning revelation that he might express the vitality of American culture through an abstract visual vocabulary. Stella's receptivity was due, in part, to a lengthy stay in Paris beginning in 1911, when he was drawn to the international avant-garde, particularly the Italian futurists.

This pastel, with its sharp, angular facets suggesting the chaotic merging of the amusement park's aural and visual characteristics, pays homage to the work of European futurists, whose dynamic forms and intense colors evoked the restless spirit of the modern age. Just outside Manhattan, Coney Island was immensely popular for its rides, sideshows, and exotic melange of fanciful architectural styles, dramatically outlined with the greatest profusion of electric lights to be found anywhere in the country. The jarring diagonal shafts that cut through this pastel suggest shooting prisms of light, which Stella rendered through vigorously applied and high-keyed color: blue and lavender dominate the bottom half of the composition, while passages of red, orange, yellow, and green appear most often in the upper sections. The series of paintings and drawings inspired by Coney Island mark Stella's public coming-of-age and prefigure his later, more iconic visual statements about America's industrial prowess. Although Stella resisted artistic classification by continuing to explore new media and subjects, his marriage of abstraction and popular culture during the mid-1910s remains one of his freshest and most provocative undertakings.

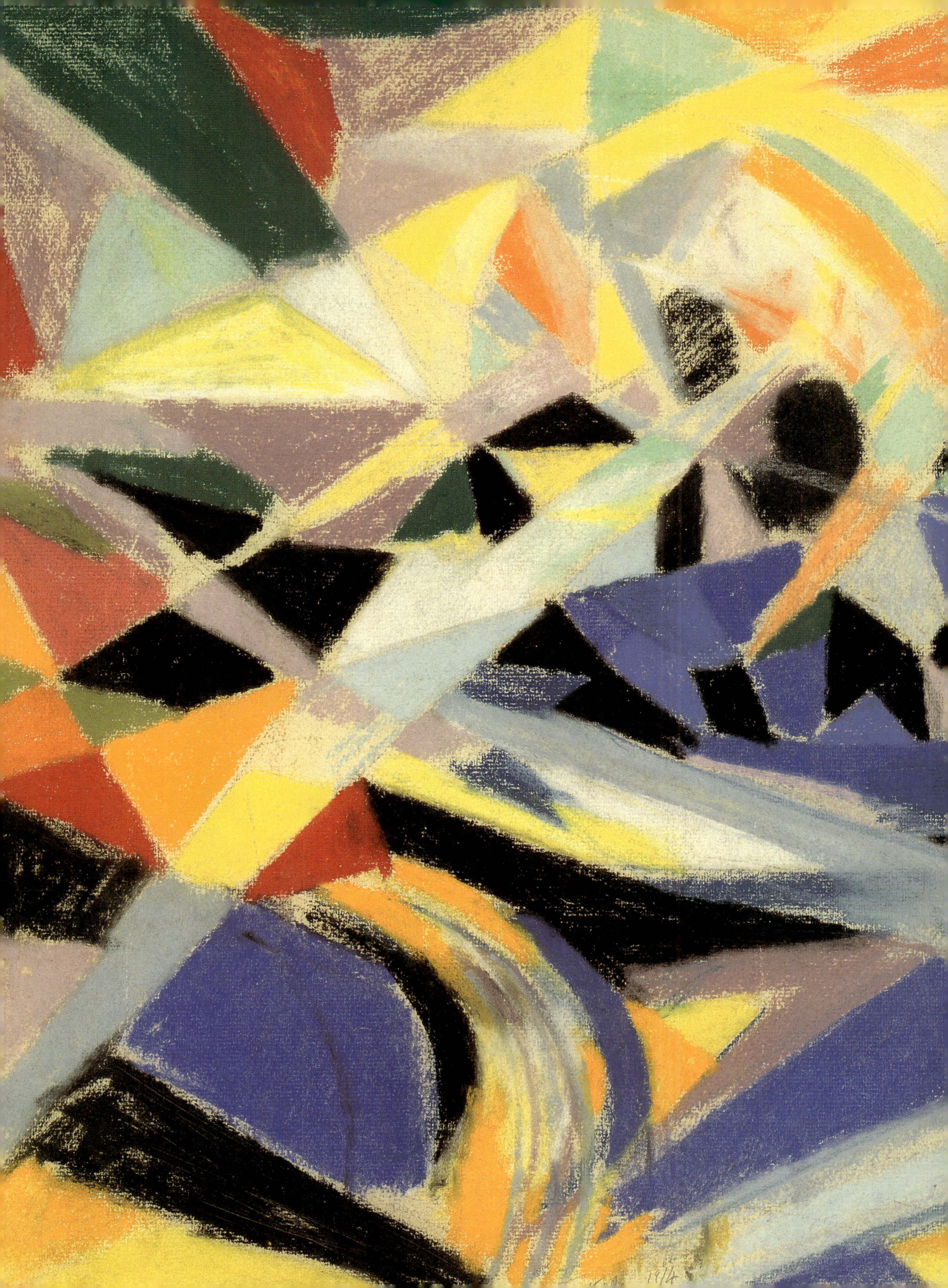

Georgia O'Keeffe
(1887–1986)

[Untitled], 1915
Charcoal on laid, cream paper
24 1/8 x 18 5/8 in. (61.3 x 47.3 cm)
Signed, dated, and inscribed, on reverse,
lower right: *#3* [by Alfred Stieglitz];
on [removed] backing: *OK* [in five-pointed star],
1915–1916 / Georgia O'Keeffe / A. Stieglitz
Partial gift of The Georgia O'Keeffe Foundation
1997.1

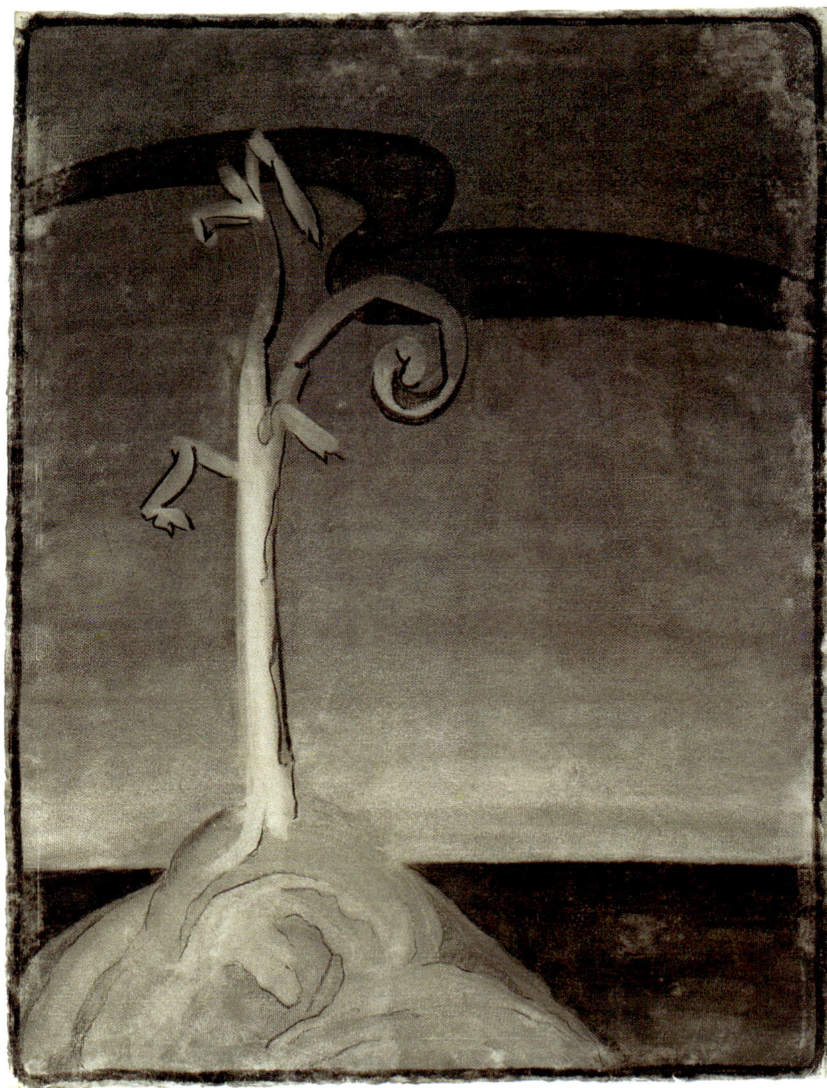

A thoughtful gesture turned into one of the more conse-
quential moments in the history of twentieth-century
American art when, in January 1916, a friend of twenty-
eight-year-old Georgia O'Keeffe showed the artist's recent
charcoal drawings to Alfred Stieglitz, the most influential
and compelling figure in New York's small avant-garde art
community. The ten charcoals were the result of O'Keeffe's
intense self-appraisal during the fall of 1915, when she
dedicated herself to purging her work of any overt influence
from such illustrious artist-instructors as William Merritt
Chase and Arthur Wesley Dow.

Feeling isolated in Columbia, South Carolina, where she
recently had taken a teaching position, O'Keeffe spread
sheets of paper on the floor of her room and tapped into her
subjective imagination. She stripped her work of color and,
as swiftly became her custom, limited landscape references
to a few key forms. The charcoals reflect not only the breakthrough expression of her personal and singular style, but
also her wide-ranging intellectual interests: avant-garde
American and European art, critical and theoretical writings on art, and the sensuous forms of the art nouveau style.

Representing O'Keeffe's seminal experimentation with
modernist abstraction, these charcoal drawings established
the groundwork for a lifetime of highly personal responses to
the natural universe. This untitled drawing depicts a taut,
plant-like form rising from a knoll within a pseudo-landscape
setting, implied by a low horizon line and a ribbon of clouds.
Even in this early sequence of works, O'Keeffe demonstrates impressive control of the medium; her application of
charcoal fluctuates from incisive black lines to
subtle gradations of gray. Stieglitz was so taken with their
frank naturalism that, in May and June 1916, he exhibited all
ten works at his 291 gallery. This exhibition not only
launched O'Keeffe's career but also instigated one of
America's more legendary artistic couplings—Stieglitz took
up residence with O'Keeffe in 1918, and they married in 1924.

Charles Demuth
(1883–1935)

Three Acrobats, 1916
Watercolor and graphite on wove, tan paper
13 x 8 in. (33.0 x 20.3 cm)
Signed and dated lower left: *C. Demuth. 1916*
1983.127

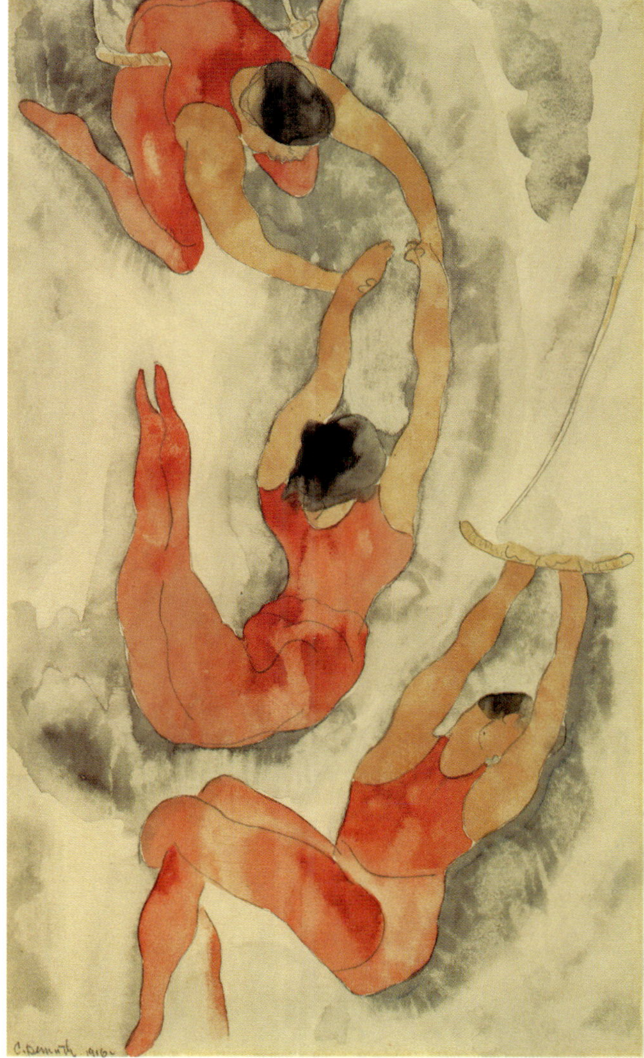

Watercolor reigned as the dominant means of artistic expression for many early-twentieth-century artists who manipulated the medium in unconventional and imaginative ways. Among the most eloquent marriages of medium and subject are the figurative watercolors Charles Demuth created between 1915 and 1919.

Demuth was an enthusiastic devotee of the popular acrobatic headliners who appeared in the circus arenas and on the vaudeville stages of the period. The artist attended their performances not only in Manhattan and Paris, Demuth's favorite bohemian haunts, but also in his native Lancaster, Pennsylvania, where he resided in the family home with his mother. Lame since childhood, Demuth relished the acrobatic acts that transcended his own earth-bound infirmity.

The artist's lively sense of color and pattern convey the visceral and aesthetic pleasure he took in the subject. He also exploits the nuances of the watercolor medium through a sophisticated control of washes, which are usually, but not always, contained by his economic use of a wiry graphite line. Lively patches of diaphanous mottled gray, created by blotting wet pigment with a textured material, cunningly reinforce the spontaneity and quickness of the performers' movements, while playing against the vivid red-orange costumes rendered in a richer, opaque application of watercolor. Despite their muscular corporeality, these synchronized figures glide with rhythmic precision and effortless agility though a space devoid of any contextual reference.

The New York City populace deemed such subjects drawn from popular entertainment to be as novel as Demuth's expressive watercolor technique. High society, however, looked askance at what they perceived to be the low rung of live performance and entertainers who worked in the seamy bars and music halls frequented by Demuth and his circle. He and other artist friends, particularly Marsden Hartley, who wrote about the performers, found these unpretentious people an exhilarating and fitting antidote to the stuffy Victorian status quo, and they warmly welcomed an association with them on the fringes of respectability.

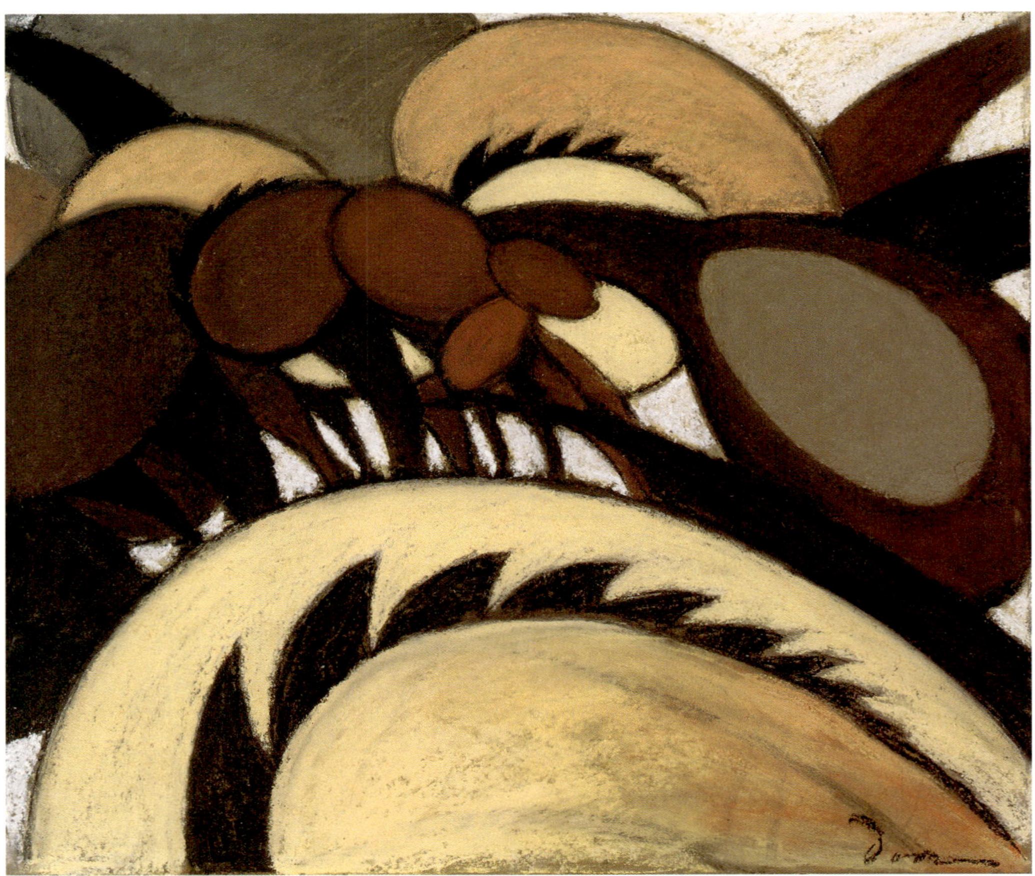

Arthur G. Dove (1880–1946)

Team of Horses, 1911 or 1912
Pastel on composition board mounted to plywood
18⅛ x 21½ in. (47 x 52.1 cm)
Signed lower right: *Dove*
1984.29

After a trip to Paris in 1908, where he absorbed the liberating ideas of European modernism and self-expression, Arthur Dove emerged as a major pioneer of American abstraction. Infusing this innovative approach was the intense spiritual connection Dove felt with nature. Working on his farm in Connecticut in the early 1910s, he created a group of ten pastels, including *Team of Horses*, which ranks among the first documented series of abstractions by an American. In these works he translates and reduces natural elements of the landscape into circles, triangles, rectangles, and other forms.

The creamy semicircles crowned with black triangles in this pastel suggest the manes of horses galloping across the landscape, while brown circles atop curving lines seem to represent trees. Other pastels from the series have a static quality, but *Team of Horses* is alive with the consonant rhythms of nature. The dynamism is implied through the upward repetition of overlapping forms, all slanting to the left as if in motion. Each form has a curving black silhouette, which accentuates the sense of rhythm. The unified palette— where umbers, ochers, siennas, blacks, and whites are care-

fully balanced—completes the cadence of the design.

Dove premiered *Team of Horses* and the other nine pastels in 1912 at the Little Galleries of the Photo-Secession, known as 291 for its address in New York. Under the direction of photographer Alfred Stieglitz, 291 was the first venue in the United States to display works by Picasso and Matisse. With its intimate space and progressive atmosphere, 291 was the ideal venue for Dove to debut his abstract style. He described the gallery in a letter to author Samuel M. Kootz: "It was a place where anything could happen. A remarkable place. People, paintings, photographs, and writings, all working as in a laboratory."

Although untitled at the time, the pastels were later assigned the group designation *The Ten Commandments* by either Stieglitz or Dove, most likely in recognition of the works' enormous stylistic innovations. Though he remained committed to his personal vision, fueled by his unwavering spirit and genuine originality, Dove's paintings proved too sophisticated for the art market, and he struggled financially his entire life.

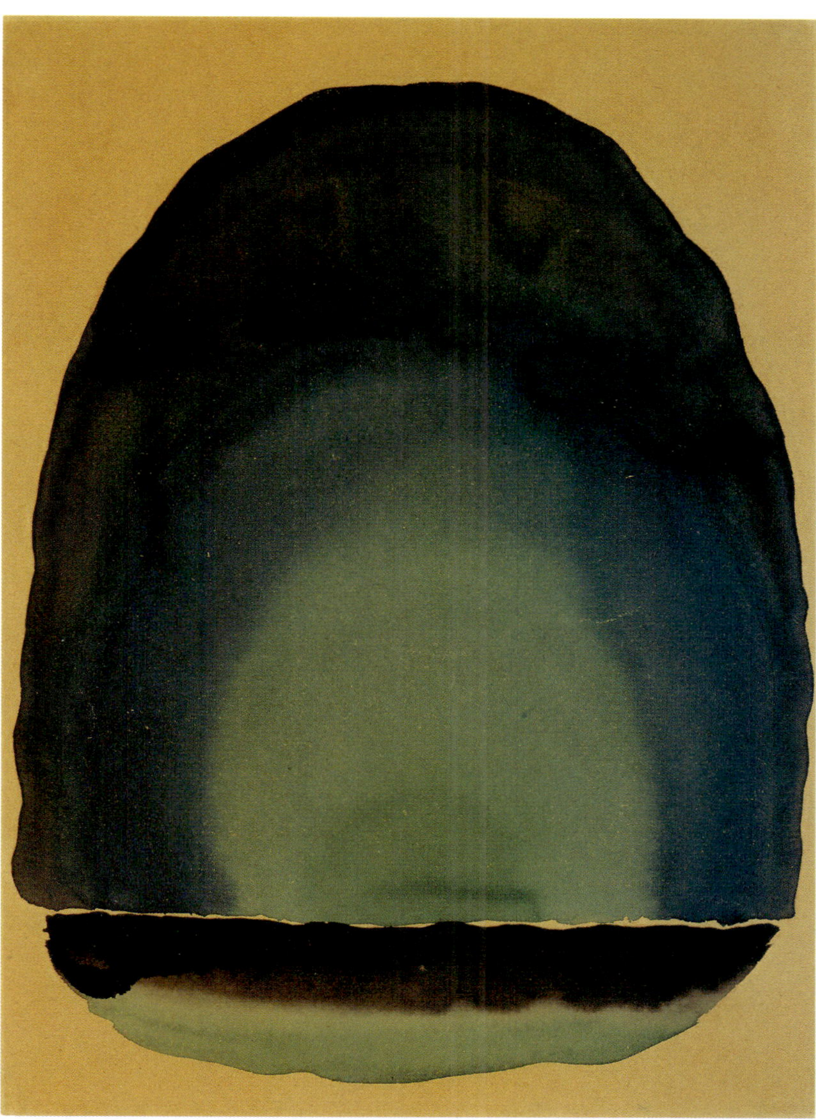

Georgia O'Keeffe
(1887–1986)

Light Coming on the Plains No. III, 1917
Watercolor on wove, beige paper [newsprint]
11⅞ x 8⅞ in. (30.2 x 22.5 cm)
Dated and inscribed on [removed] label:
Light Coming on the Plains/1917/No. III
1966.31

Not long after Georgia O'Keeffe created a group of black-and-white charcoal drawings that gave rise to her unique artistic voice, she began to incorporate vibrant color into her work. Among her earliest efforts is a brilliant series of watercolors produced in the Texas Panhandle. With several teaching positions behind her, O'Keeffe had returned to New York in early 1916 to resume her art studies with the famed teacher Arthur Wesley Dow. His emphasis on the balance of form, color, and dark and light, over precise rendition, is evident in her series *Light Coming on the Plains I, II, and III*, three watercolors made in Canyon, Texas, where she would spend one and one-half years teaching art at West Texas State Normal College. These watercolors represent her liberation from conventional artistic methods and her euphoric response to the land and atmosphere of the plains.

Using a remarkably controlled technique, O'Keeffe applied watercolor to a dry sheet, exploiting the medium's liquid and sensuous properties by allowing the pigment to dictate crisp parameters without benefit of graphite under-drawing. The resulting reductive form summarized O'Keeffe's emotional response to sunlight peeking over the austere Texas plains, a vast landscape that recalled the freedom of her rural Wisconsin childhood. Texas' limitless spaces and evocative natural light seemed to lift her spirits and provide solace to this somewhat notorious figure, known in Canyon for her blithe independence. Among her perceived eccentricities was a fondness for staying out all night to experience dawn, when the effects of light were the most transitory and ephemeral. She translated this experience into subtle tonal gradations of green and blue watercolor, imperceptibly blended on paper to form gently contoured concentric rings. Her simple forms, rich in their allusions to natural cycles, hover between pure sensation and visual fact, no less intensely observed for their nearly pure abstraction.

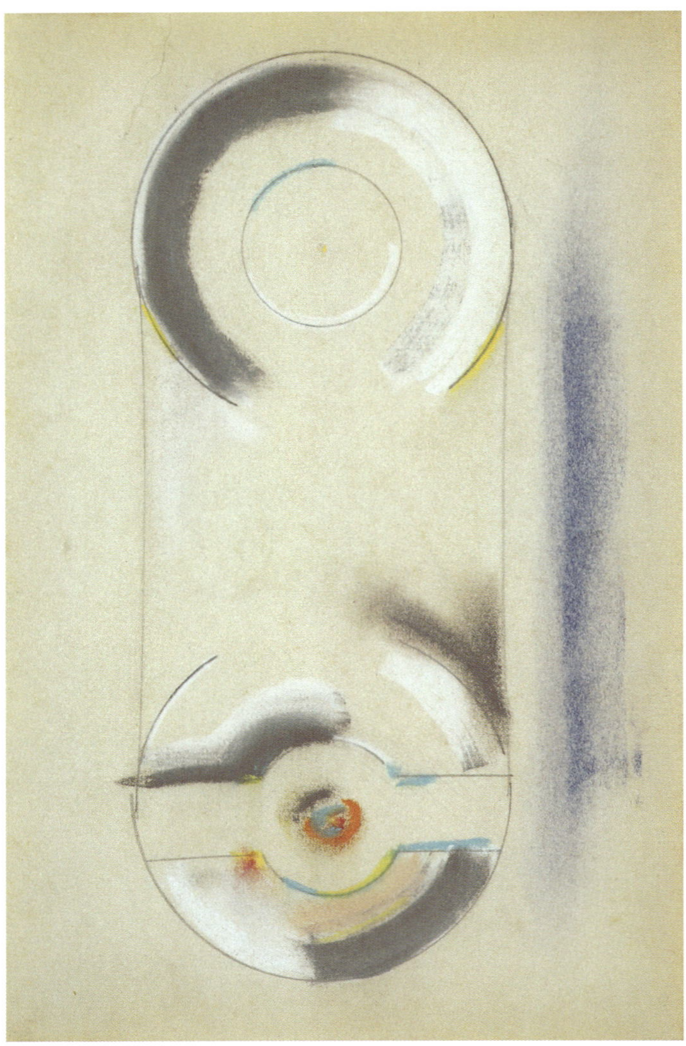

Morton Livingston Schamberg
(1881–1918)

Composition, 1916
Pastel and graphite on laid, cream paper
9¾ x 6⅝ in. (24.8 x 16.8 cm)
1983.173

In 1916 Morton Livingston Schamberg became one of the first American artists to consider the aesthetic possibilities of the ordinary machine when he isolated industrial fragments in a series of thirty delicate and provocatively colored pastel drawings. A lifelong resident of Philadelphia and graduate of the Pennsylvania Academy of the Fine Arts, Schamberg acquired a thorough overview of modern art through his travels to Europe, particularly Paris, and, in 1913, his attendance at the Armory Show in New York City, the first major exhibition of modernism in the United States. Schamberg swiftly became well read in avant-garde theory and published writings on the subject as his work evolved from a cubist rearrangement of forms into this kind of spare abstraction.

Printing and textile equipment catalogues served as sources for the spare forms Schamberg extracted from their original context, possibly owing to his brother-in-law's career as a stocking manufacturer. Still, even the barest definition alludes to an object's original function. Schamberg depicted the pulley system in *Composition* by outlining its wheels and belt in precise graphite lines and circles, which recall his training in draftsmanship as an architectural student at the University of Pennsylvania in the early 1900s. To these geometrical shapes, the artist applied an innovative, pastel palette: rich, arcing swaths of gray and white accented with brisk touches of intense pink, orange, and turquoise. Softly blurred, these forms evoke synchronized motion.

In subject matter and style, this series of pastels, which came to light only in the early 1980s, anticipates the advent of machine-inspired precisionism at the end of the decade. Tragically, Schamberg did not live to develop the remarkable promise evidenced in these works on paper; he fell victim to the influenza epidemic of 1918, dying two days before his thirty-seventh birthday.

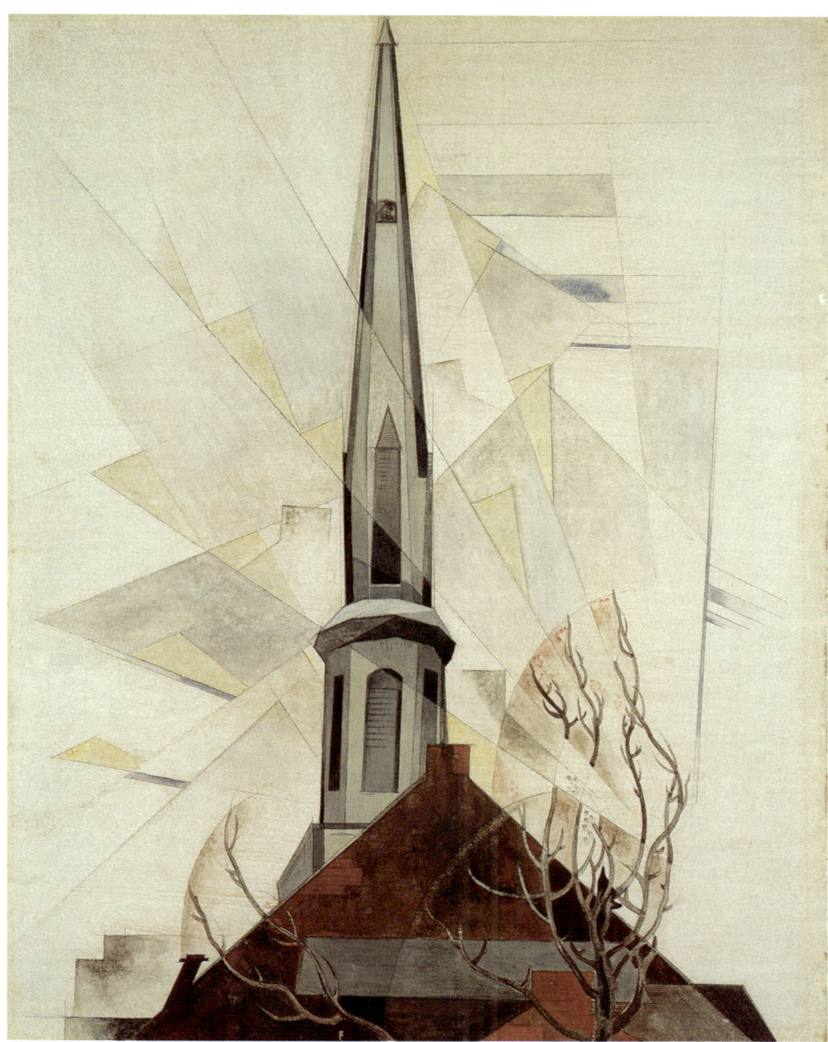

Charles Demuth
(1883–1935)

In the Province #7, 1920
Tempera, watercolor, and graphite on composition board
20 x 16 in. (50.8 x 40.7 cm)
Signed, dated, and inscribed, lower center: *C. Dem*[uth]
Lancaster Pa; on reverse, upper center: *In the Province #7-*
C. Demuth Lancaster Pa 1920
1982.55

In the aftermath of World War I, the United States entered a period of reflection and reassessment. Leading cultural observers called for a casting aside of Europe's powerful influence as the progenitor of the twentieth-century avant-garde, maintaining that American artists should address the life and traditions of their own country. One outcome of this nativism was the merger of modern forms of expression with uniquely indigenous subjects.

Charles Demuth's *In the Province #7* depicts the steeple of St. John's German Reformed Church, one of many that dotted the town of Lancaster, Pennsylvania, and just three blocks from where the artist lived with his mother. "The province" was Demuth's ironic appellation for his hometown and a term he bantered about within his circle of writers and artists in Paris and New York City. Even so, Demuth's emotional roots ran deep into the community that remained his primary residence.

Both St. John's Church and the Demuth family shared a common heritage, due to the influx of German religious sects to Pennsylvania during the eighteenth century. While the artist was not religious, his mother was a devout member of the Trinity Lutheran Church, whose steeple loomed over the Demuth's backyard and became one of the artist's favored motifs. In 1920, the year he executed *In the Province #7*, Demuth experienced acute diabetes attacks, which eventually forced him to return home from more cosmopolitan art centers. In contrast to his earlier, more fluid style, Demuth began to explore careful arrangements of precise architectural forms that echoed the schematic and faceted qualities of cubism. Here, diagonal rays, some radiating from the bare tree branches, enliven the surrounding space as they transverse the colonial revival steeple, which was added to St. John's around 1880. Isolated, towering architectural elements would grow even more monumental in Demuth's work as he turned his attention to Lancaster's industrial environs. Reconciled to life in small-town America and fully aware that he was heeding the call for compelling and innovative expressions of a nation's psyche, Demuth continued to create images that resonate powerfully with his affinity for place.

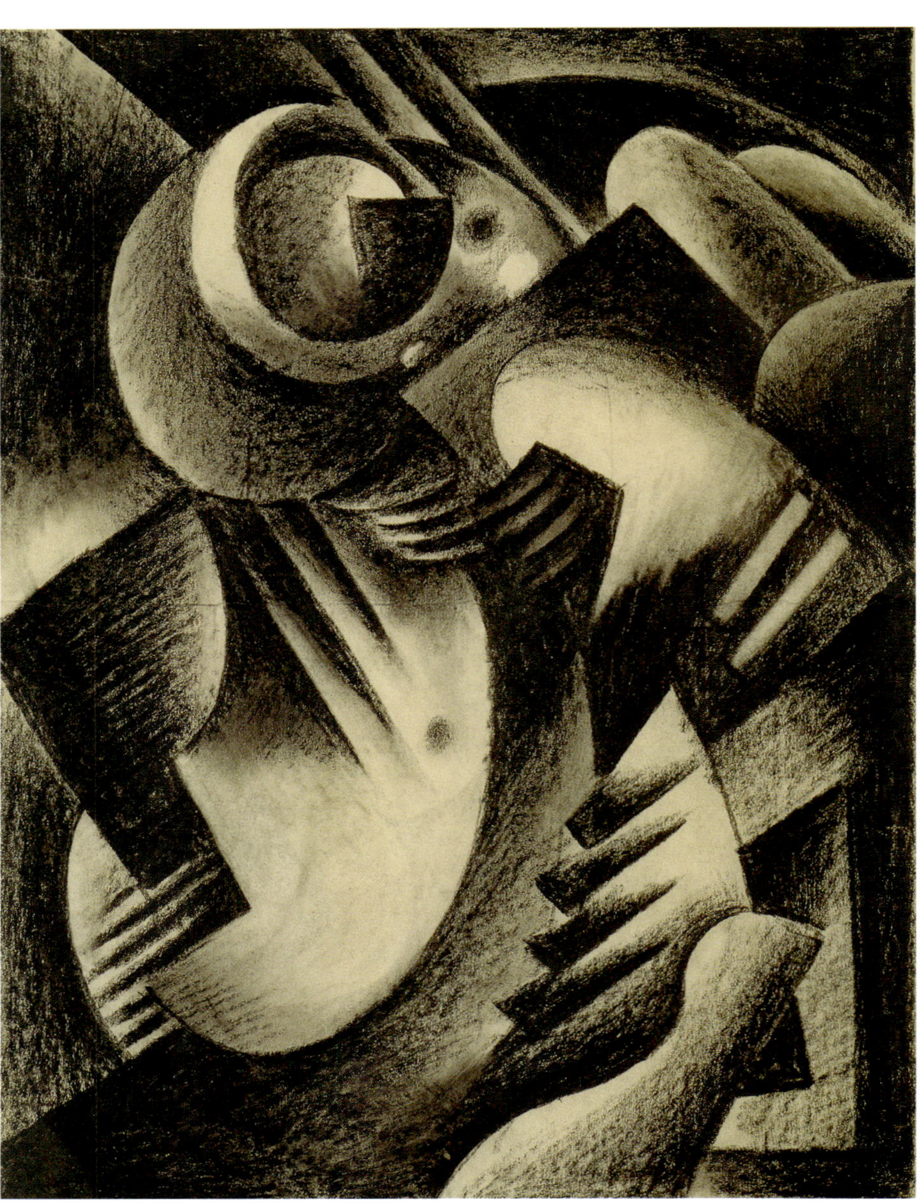

Jan Matulka
(1890–1972)

Cubist Abstraction, 1923
Conté crayon on wove, cream paper
12 x 8½ in. (30.5 x 21.6 cm)
1984.17

Modernist art created during the 1920s did not attract the same shocked, sometimes scandalous reception that it was given in the previous decade. This is not to imply that such art was any less vital. In fact, post-war artists like Jan Matulka continued to find sustenance on the cutting edge of artistic theory and practice within the still-thriving avant-garde circles of New York and Paris. During an extended stay in Europe from 1920–24, Matulka established a studio in the French capital and made regular visits to Prague, which boasted its own modernist tradition and was located near the Bohemian home he had left with his parents in 1907.

A group of black-and-white drawings Matulka made in France number among the most powerful and abstract works of his career. They are distinguished—like this one—by overlapping forms, which impart volume, depth, and solidity to edgy, yet formally unified, statements. Taking his direction from cubism, which continued to flourish in Paris, Matulka made rich and varied allusions to real objects through evocative shapes that reference celestial orbs, the human figure, and musical imagery. Matulka's own passion for music was fundamental to his life in Paris, where he frequented the Ballets Russes and enthusiastically followed the controversial dissonance of composer Igor Stravinsky. The combination of curvilinear elements and striated patterns here recall the guitar imagery adopted by the French cubists. Suggestions of musical notes, as well as the overall sense of cacophony, reference the elusive synthesis of sound and sight hailed by early-twentieth-century modernists.

In 1924 Matulka returned to New York City. He spent the rest of the decade producing work that combined abstraction and representation, and he carried the banner of modernism at the Art Students League, where he was an influential teacher. But the 1930s saw a marked and enduring decline in his productivity. He would never again recapture the inspiration he enjoyed in Paris when his innovative work placed him at the forefront of modernism.

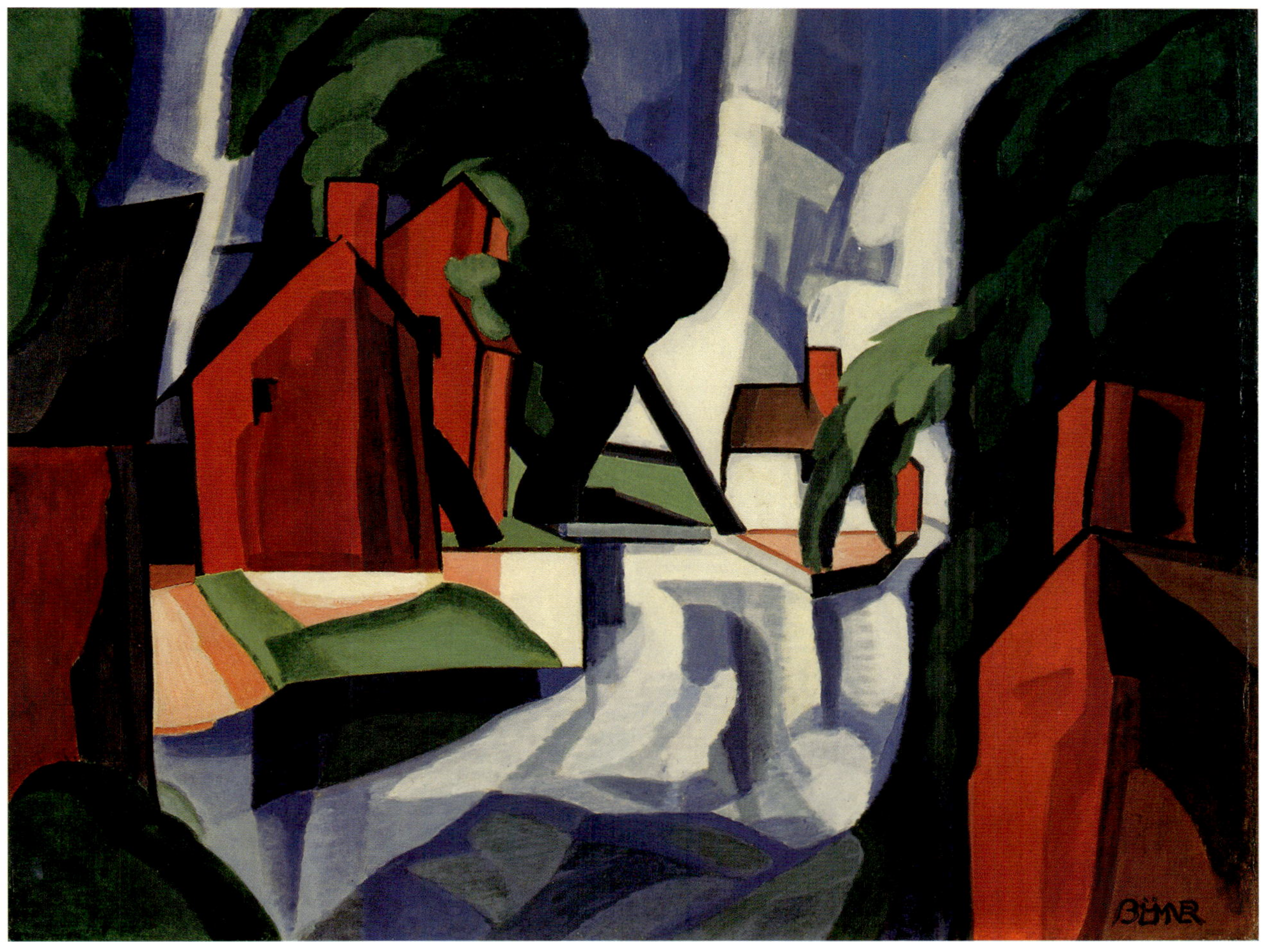

Oscar Bluemner (1867–1938)

Blue Day, 1930
Casein on paper mounted to layered paperboard
15 x 20⅛ in. (38.1 x 51.1 cm)
Signed lower right: *Blüemner* [monogram]
1981.65

Oscar Bluemner's fascination with the spiritual and emotional connotations of color gave rise to a singular vision that distinguished this Prussian-born artist from others in the vanguard. In *Blue Day* he adopts a traditional subject from the canon of American art: a carefully composed view of a small town harmoniously tucked into the surrounding countryside. Unlike previous landscapists, however, Bluemner charged this innocuous scene with raw emotion, greatly exaggerating the organic rhythms and true palette of the scene. *Blue Day* portrays an area of northeastern New Jersey where the artist and his family resided between 1916 and 1926. Upon the death of his wife in 1926, Bluemner moved to Massachusetts, but the New Jersey terrain continued to be a source of solace for the often-troubled artist. *Blue Day* portrays the red brick buildings of Boontown, situated along the Morris Canal, a waterway completed in 1831 to support the local iron ore industry.

In his diary Bluemner recorded *Blue Day*'s intense and sensuous colors: buildings of vermilion, sky and water of lapis lazuli, and vegetation of malachite. A blue-and-white swath cutting across the composition indicates water spilling into the foreground, an expressive element contributing to the pulsating, almost anthropomorphic, whole. To heighten the colors' brilliance, Bluemner made the water-based pigment opaque by adding casein, an experiment he attempted for the first time in *Blue Day*. This method allowed him to approximate the effect of oil paint and enhance the permanence of fragile watercolor.

Bluemner found multiple layers of meaning in these vivid colors, his reading informed by a close study of philosophy, art theory, history, psychology, and music. He associated red with vitality and power, green with repose, and blue with coolness and space. But these elusive and complex meanings ensured that the reception of his work would be tepid. Declining health and lack of financial and professional success contributed to his suicide in 1938.

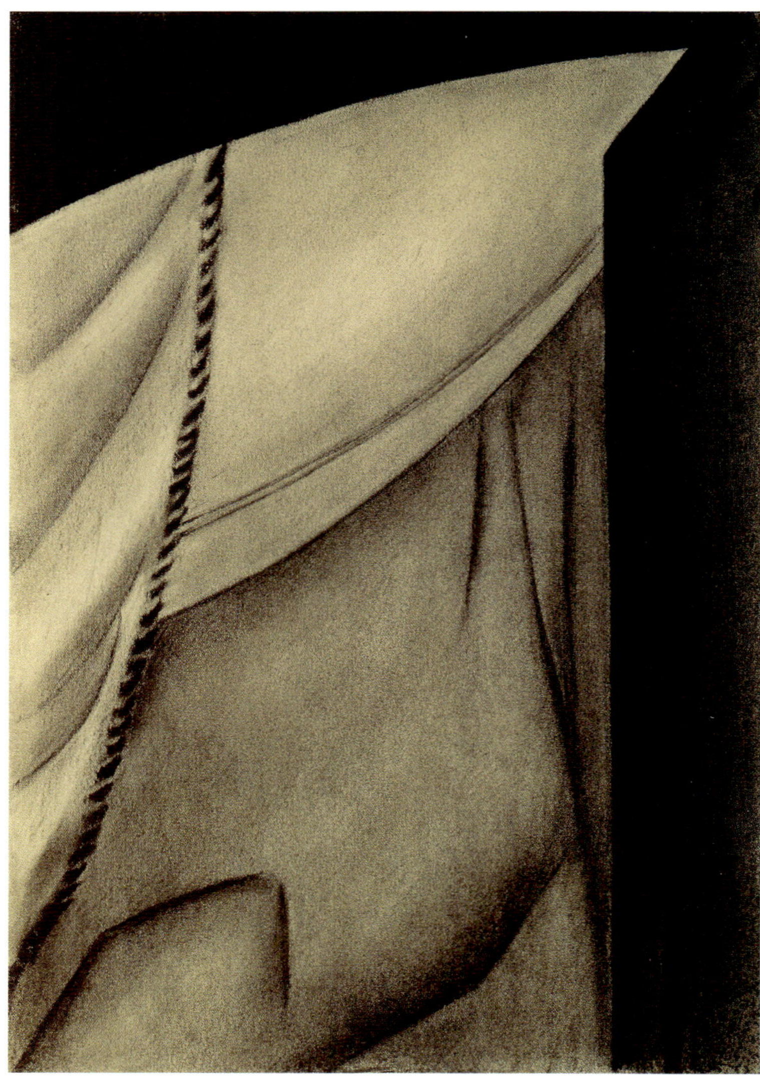

Helen Torr
(1886–1967)

Through the Door, ca. 1935
Charcoal on wove, off-white paper
14 x 10 in. (35.6 x 25.4 cm)
1985.24

A few years after attending the Pennsylvania Academy of the Fine Arts on scholarship, Helen Torr settled in Westport, Connecticut, with her husband, Clive Weed, a political cartoonist. There, she met artist Arthur Dove. The two fell in love and created a scandal when they left their spouses to live together in 1921. Dove nicknamed Torr "Reds" for her curly red hair and supported her artistic aims. But Torr was self-defeating and easily discouraged about her art. Hoping to exhibit with Dove in 1927, she recorded in her journal that she was "sunk" that Alfred Stieglitz had said her works were "too frail . . . to show with Arthur." Torr exhibited only twice during her lifetime: in a 1927 group exhibition arranged by Georgia O'Keeffe and at Stieglitz's gallery, An American Place, in 1933.

Helen Torr's charcoal drawings, wherein she often abandoned her representational style and explored abstract designs, are arguably her most provocative works. Her application of the medium in *Through the Door* yields a rich velvety texture, like folds in drapery. The rope to the left of the image and the beckoning door on the right serve as visual anchors for the otherwise amorphous shapes. During the 1920s, Torr lived with Dove on a sailboat named *Mona,* which inspired a small number of nautically themed charcoals. While elements in *Through the Door* echo lines and sails, the drawing mostly invokes mystery; the door is open, yet obstructed by the seemingly impenetrable layers of sweeping cloth. Torr had yet to receive any lasting recognition at the time she produced this work, and the doorway's blocked entrance may reflect the artist's feelings about her stalled career. An entry from Torr's journal in 1935, "Made a drawing looking through the door," provides a literal reference for the title and perspective in this drawing, and yet the subject remains particularly enigmatic. After Dove's death in 1946, Torr never worked again, establishing this unique drawing as a rare and poignant memento of her forsaken talent.

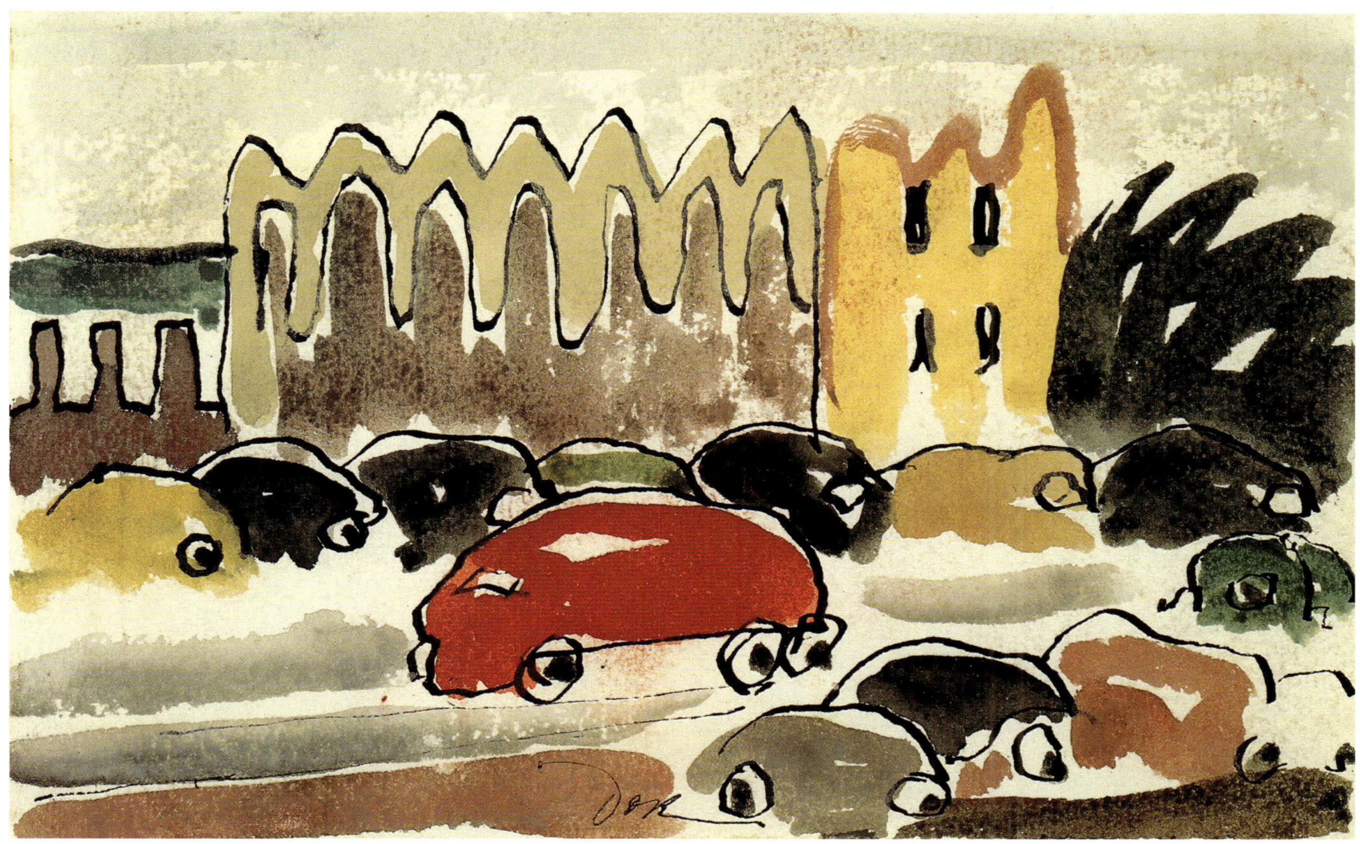

Arthur G. Dove (1880–1946)

Exchange Street, Geneva, 1938
Ink and transparent and opaque watercolor on wove, buff paper
5½ x 9 in. (14.0 x 22.8 cm)
Signed lower center: *Dove*
1982.57

In contrast to his abstract style in *Team of Horses*, Arthur Dove drew *Exchange Street, Geneva* in a representational manner to capture this charming and spontaneous view of his hometown. From habit, Dove combed his immediate surroundings for inspiration, often using watercolors to sketch ideas quickly and later expanding upon those ideas in oil paintings. Eventually he recognized these small watercolors as works of art in themselves and incorporated a select few in his exhibitions. *Exchange Street, Geneva* was one of the small jewels he displayed in a 1938 solo exhibition at Alfred Stieglitz's New York gallery, An American Place. Its fluid design imparts the artist's dexterous handling of various media, especially pen and ink. The latter were Dove's primary tools in his work as a freelance commercial illustrator, an occupation he loathed but one which often provided his only income. Here, Dove uses black pen lines in a loose, generalized manner, describing the scene with a caricature-like appearance. He brushed the parked cars and skyline with a vibrant palette of leafy greens, grays, yellows, and crimson reds that animate the composition.

It was the death of his mother in 1933 that forced Dove to return to his hometown of Geneva, New York, to settle debts on the family's property: farmland, houses, brick and tile plants, and a commercial block. Hesitant to go there, Dove described his feelings in a letter to his close friend Stieglitz: "There is something terrible about 'Up State' to me. . . . It is like walking on the bottom underwater." Upon arriving, Dove and his wife, Helen Torr, chose to live on farmland bordering Exchange Street in a house without electricity or running water. To opt for such an ascetic life was not unusual for the artist, who in the 1920s had lived without utilities aboard his sailboat, *Mona*. Moreover, the privacy of the farm meant Dove could paint freely outdoors.

Shortly before moving to Centerport, Long Island, Dove created this exuberant watercolor on Exchange Street in Geneva, perhaps as a keepsake of his birthplace. Ironically, his reluctant five-year stay in Geneva was one of the most productive periods of his career. Shortly thereafter he was stricken with heart problems and kidney disease, and he would never be as prolific again.

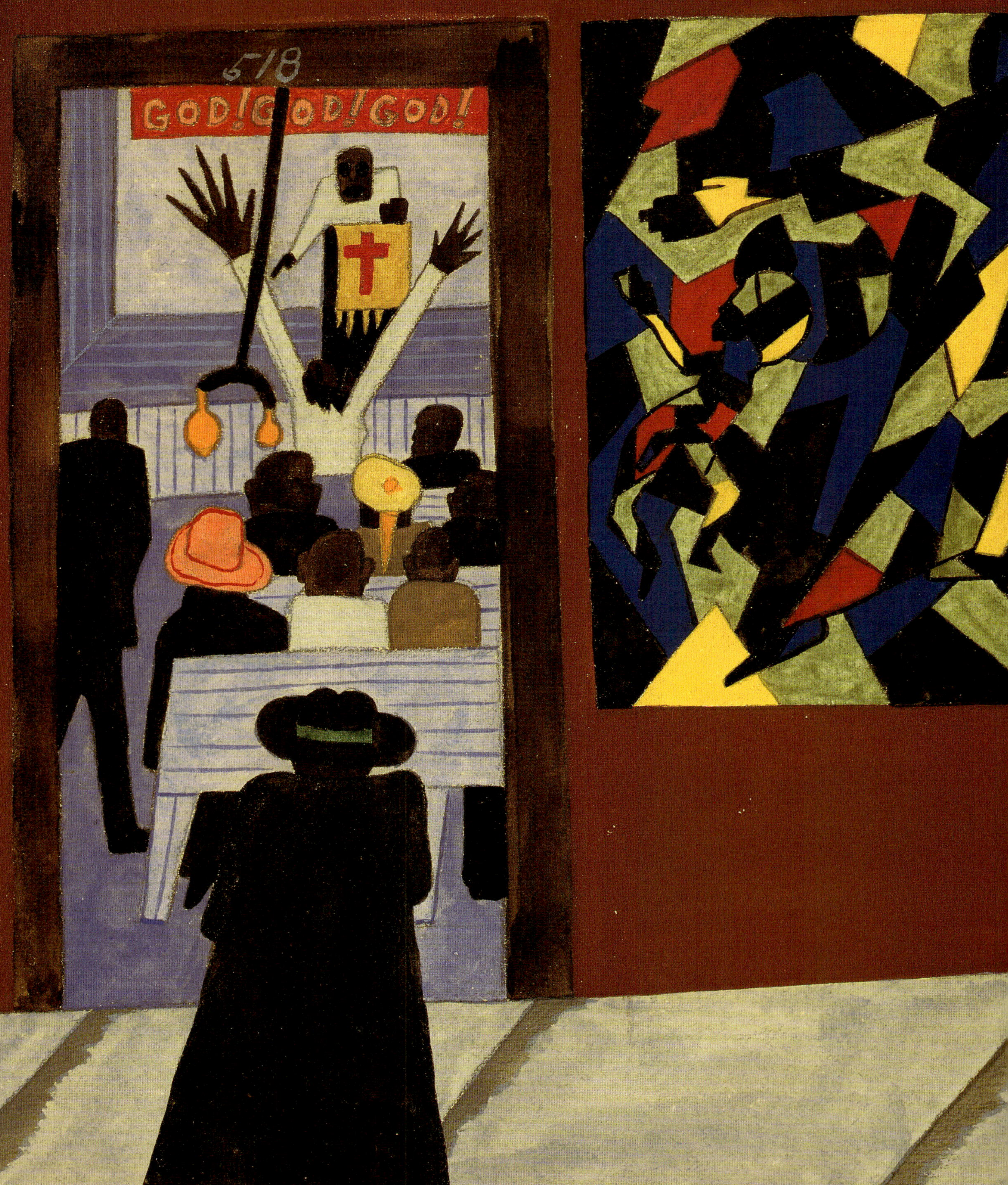

CHURCH·OF·
518
GOD! GOD! GOD!

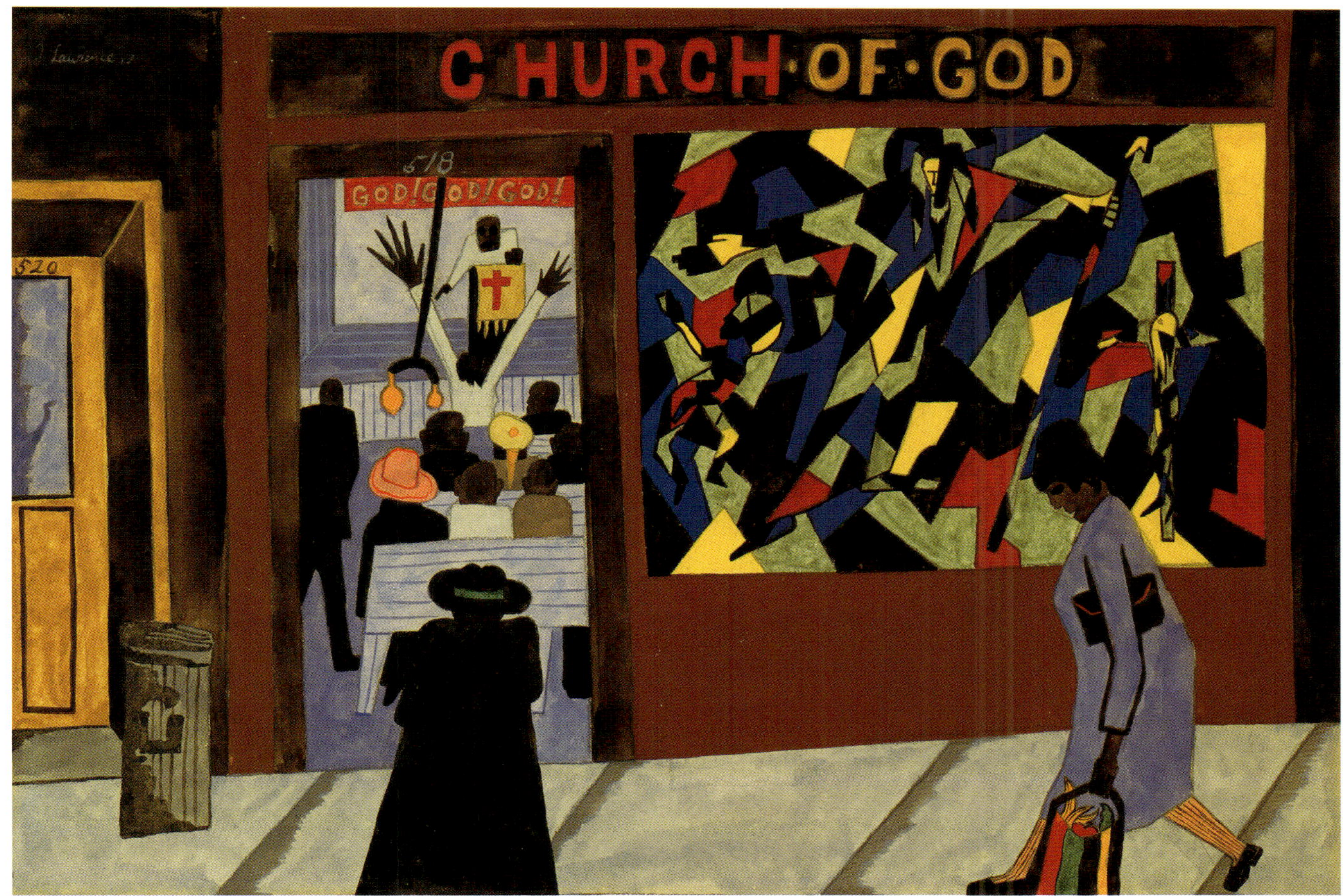

Jacob Lawrence (1917–2000)

There are many churches in Harlem. The people are very religious., 1943
Transparent and opaque watercolor on wove, buff paper
15½ x 22½ in. (39.4 x 57.2 cm)
Signed and dated upper left: *J. Lawrence 43*
Copyright 1943, Jacob Lawrence
1987.94

Despite the upheavals brought about by the depression and World War II, artistic vigor and ethnic pride continued to inspire many creative achievements in Harlem following its cultural renaissance of the 1920s. Through his masterful series of thirty hard-edged and vividly colored opaque watercolors entitled *Harlem*, Jacob Lawrence returned to the impoverished, yet pulsating, neighborhood that had embraced him upon his arrival there in 1930. In 1942 and 1943, only in his mid-twenties and already attracting professional recognition, Lawrence created this visual narrative of everyday life in his old neighborhood, depicting its inhabitants with a degree of authenticity born of experience. Together, this string of simple stories about education, social life, labor, and the daily struggle to survive afford a comprehensive look at the neighborhood's joys and sorrows.

This watercolor depicts one of the numerous storefront churches that multiplied during the depression and were integral to the daily life of the community. These churches offered an escapism that primarily attracted the poorest and least educated to their congregations. Lawrence's image may allude to the cynical attitude taken by some writers and other intellectuals that Harlem's storefront preachers were opportunists. The minister's impassioned exegesis touches the standing figure, whose fervent response is described through her expressive, outstretched arms and oversized hands. The social commentary is subtle, however, for Lawrence focused on the visual complexity of the stage-like setting: the angular facets of a colored glass window and, in the foreground, two women in silhouette. One, silently dedicated to her shopping task, may celebrate the achievements of the artist's hard-working mother, who single-handedly raised Lawrence and his two siblings.

When the *Harlem* series was exhibited at the Downtown Gallery in 1943, it was praised for its humanizing perspective on a Manhattan neighborhood, albeit one unseen and even feared by many New Yorkers. To the critics of the day, the artist offered a stylized sociological study free of sentimentality but tinged with hope.

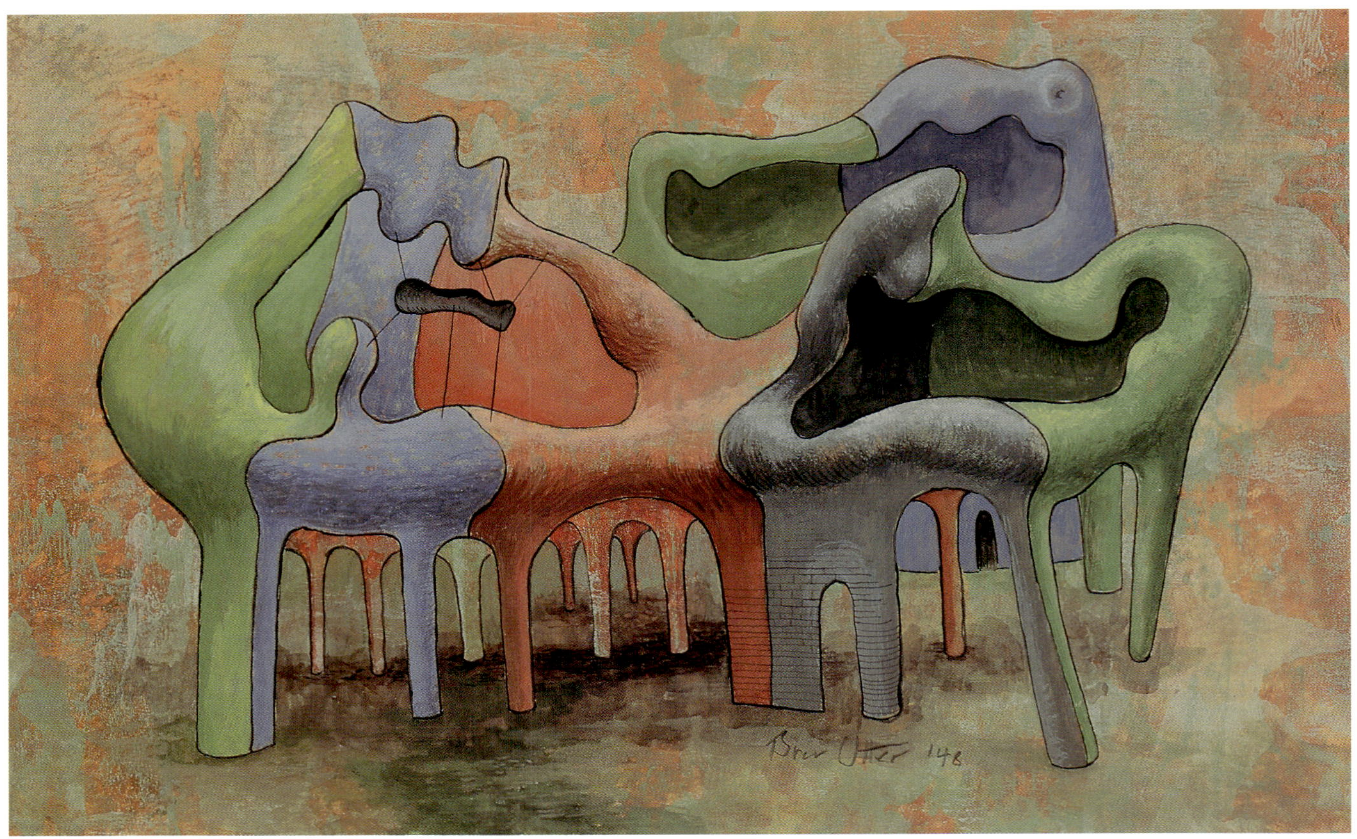

Bror Utter (1913–1993)

[Untitled], 1948
Opaque watercolor and ink on paperboard
10¾ x 16 in. (27.3 x 40.7 cm)
Signed and dated lower right: *Bror Utter '48*
1991.6

American artists who followed a modernist path during the 1930s and 1940s practiced as many different strains of surrealism as did the European artists who had instigated the movement. Some, like Bror Utter, working in a regional pocket of exploration and innovation, expressed a dreamlike state of unconscious thought through enigmatic architectonic and biomorphic shapes. A resident of Fort Worth, Texas, where he was active as an art teacher and practicing artist, Utter exhibited his unique vision through a personal store of imagery—ranging from underwater fantasies to pharmaceutical cabinets—that he reworked repeatedly in oils, watercolors, drawings, and etchings.

This untitled gouache displays the artist's fine sense of form, sensitive use of color, and ambiguity of scale that characterize his best work. Set against a mottled background, a series of arches, broadly segmented into pale red, green, and blue elements, supports a mass of undulating forms suggestive of giant organisms. The three-dimensional illusion of shadowy, arched passages, some scored into individual building blocks, reflects the artist's fascination with Roman aqueducts and the spare architectural spaces of early Italian panel painting. One distant archway remains dark and opaque, perhaps signifying yet another spatial dimension containing surreal forms.

Utter worked within a small, dynamic group of artists now known as the "Fort Worth Circle," all of whom were connected socially as well as artistically during the 1940s and 1950s. These artists, a number of whom had studied either in Europe or New York, initially gathered around the intaglio printing press owned by a member of the group. Increasingly, their work gravitated toward both allegorical fantasy and experimentation with organic, abstract forms. In 1944 New York's Weyhe Gallery featured Utter's works in *Six Texas Painters*, an exhibition that brought this striking, regional material to the attention of a broad section of that city's art community.

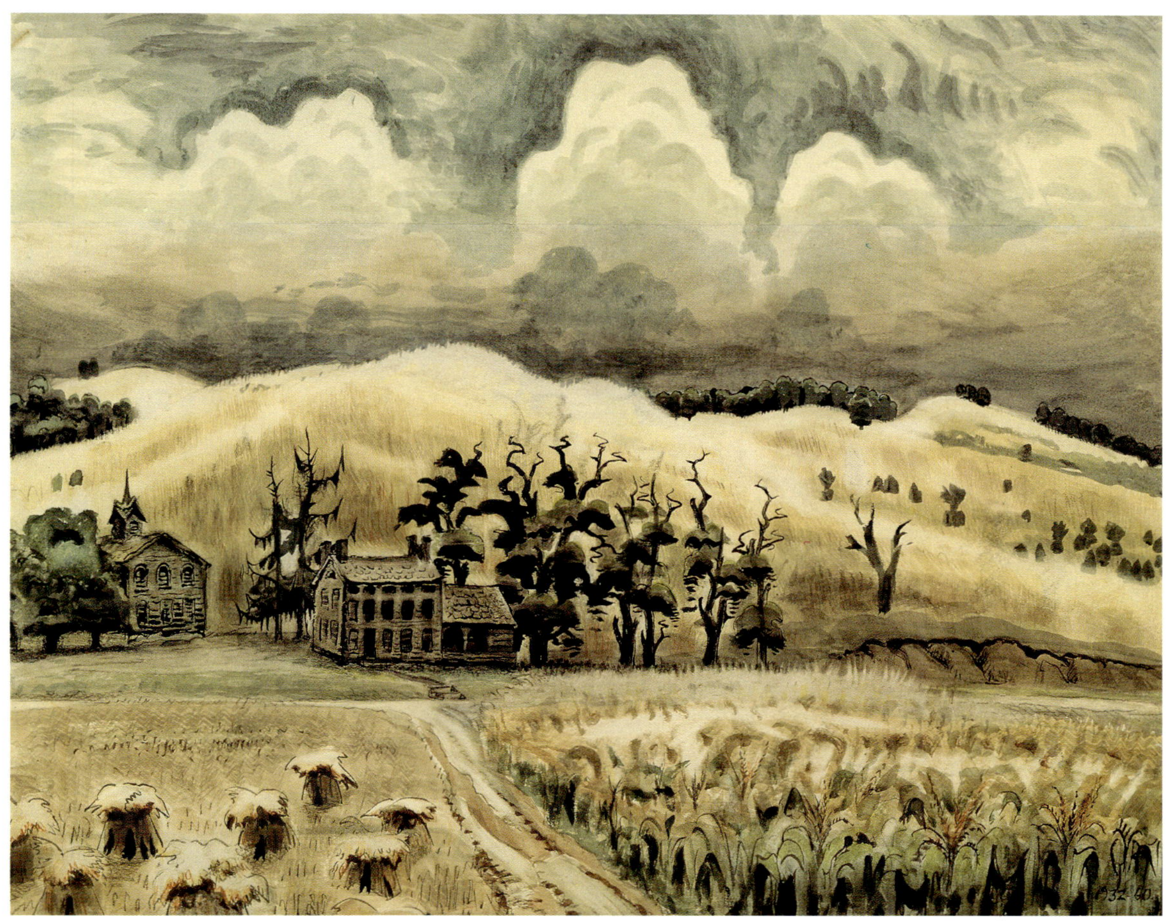

Charles E. Burchfield (1893–1967)

Bearded Hills in August, 1932–60
Watercolor, black and red crayon on wove,
off-white paper mounted to board
21⅛ x 26⅞ in. (53.6 x 68.3 cm)
Signed and dated lower right: *CEB* [monogram]/*1932–60*
1984.38

Charles Burchfield imparts an eerie foreboding to the small towns and rural landscape of Ohio, his birthplace, and the Buffalo, New York, area, his residence for much of his adult life. This singular vision was rooted in his deep affinity for these classic American venues. During a sketching outing in 1932, Burchfield came upon vast cornfields surrounding an abandoned farm near Chaffee, New York. His journal entry extolls the gentle forms of the rolling hills, the pungent smell of the rich earth, and the agreeable sounds of insects, revealing his complete sensory immersion in the experience. From his elevated vantage point, Burchfield describes the broad vista as "bearded hill country." This colloquialism referred to the corn's silky tassels, whose soft, undulating forms the artist likened to a giant's shaggy hair. His diary observations are also tinged with poignancy. He speculates about the former inhabitants of the derelict homestead, conjuring up wistful reminiscences of childhood and his own extended family gathered around the dinner table.

Burchfield depicts the stylized cornstalks and austere trees in muted colors, creating a paradoxically forlorn image to record his firsthand encounter with a bountiful landscape filled with mature corn. Three decades later, Burchfield reinforced the scene's brooding quality by enlarging the composition with a horizontal strip of paper containing thunderheads. This ominous motif runs throughout his work and serves as a symbiotic counterfoil to the forms of the terrain. This "reconstruction," a method Burchfield began in the 1940s, accentuated the effect of the expressive cloud configurations that now overwhelm the desolate remnants of human habitation. Burchfield's poetic rendering speaks to the passage of time, memory, and loss as perceived by an artist then in his mid-sixties and in failing health.

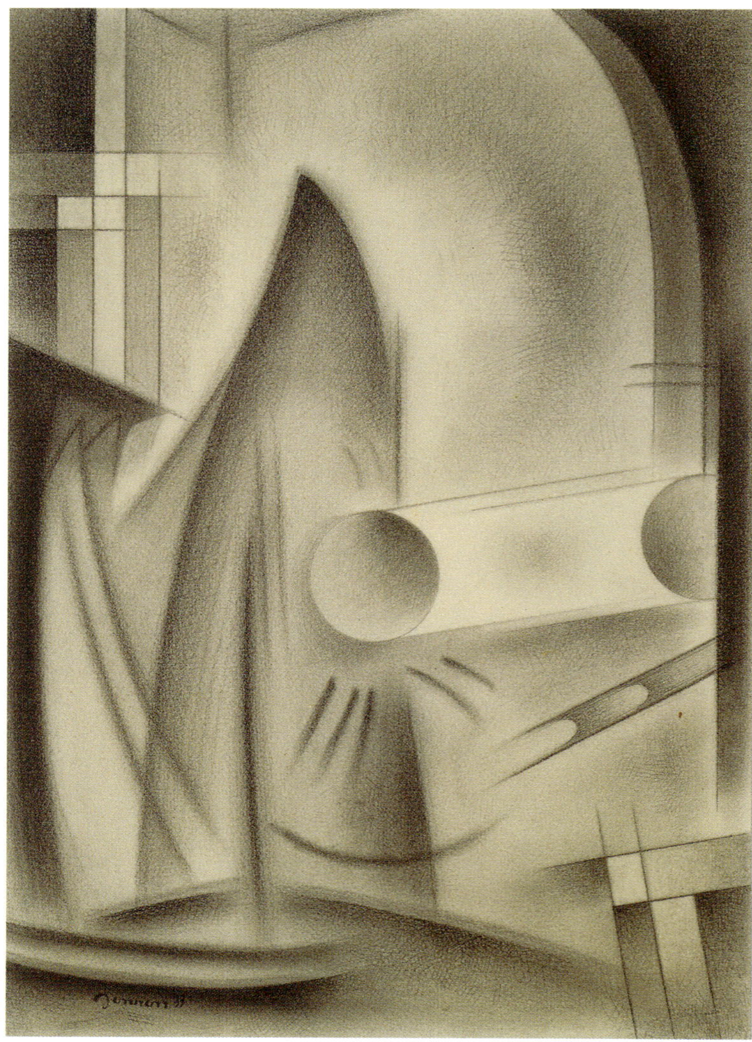

Raymond Jonson
(1891–1982)

Eclipse, 1933
Graphite on wove, off-white paper
17 x 12⅝ in. (43.2 x 32.1 cm)
Signed, dated, and inscribed, lower left: *Jonson 33*;
lower left in margin: *FIXED/JAN. 1933 4* [encircled] *ECLIPSE*
1989.8

For Raymond Jonson, art was a way of expressing the mystical. Inspired by Wassily Kandinsky's method of seeking visual forms for emotional states, Jonson strove to find pictorial equivalents for metaphysical realities, stating that art's role is to "bring about the fusion of matter with spirit." To achieve this goal, Jonson would often systematically explore an idea, such as natural rhythms in the landscape, through a series of works.

Eclipse is one of a sequence of twenty-six graphite drawings in which he sought a unifying expression for the collective relationships of the earth, sun, and sky. As the title infers, Jonson seems to be applying his well-crafted geometry to describe the cycle in which one celestial body obscures another. Distinct grids in the corners provide underlying structure as he renders patterns of movement among the shapes. The central circle collides with the tall conical shape, sparking apparent sources of energy. Highly ordered and deductive, this intricate drawing demonstrates the artist's complex style and is among his earliest nonrepresentational work.

Only after years of methodical contemplation did Jonson actually arrive at his desired method of expression. One influential event occurred early in his career when Arthur Dove's traveling exhibition of untitled abstractions, later known as *The Ten Commandments*, arrived in 1912 at the W. Scott Thurber Galleries in Chicago, where Jonson was studying art. Dove spoke at the gallery, describing his radically new works as feelings recalled "purely through their form and color." While it would be two more decades before he reached pure abstraction, Jonson, like Dove, would ultimately seek to convey a transcendent concept through shapes and hues.

In 1924 Jonson relocated to Santa Fe, where the expansive sky and rugged terrain provided the ideal setting for his analytical studies. Due to his remote location, however, Jonson did not receive the critical attention his contemporaries enjoyed in New York. Today, his work affirms his crucial role in American modernism: the translation into art of the seemingly inexpressible relationship between mind and matter.

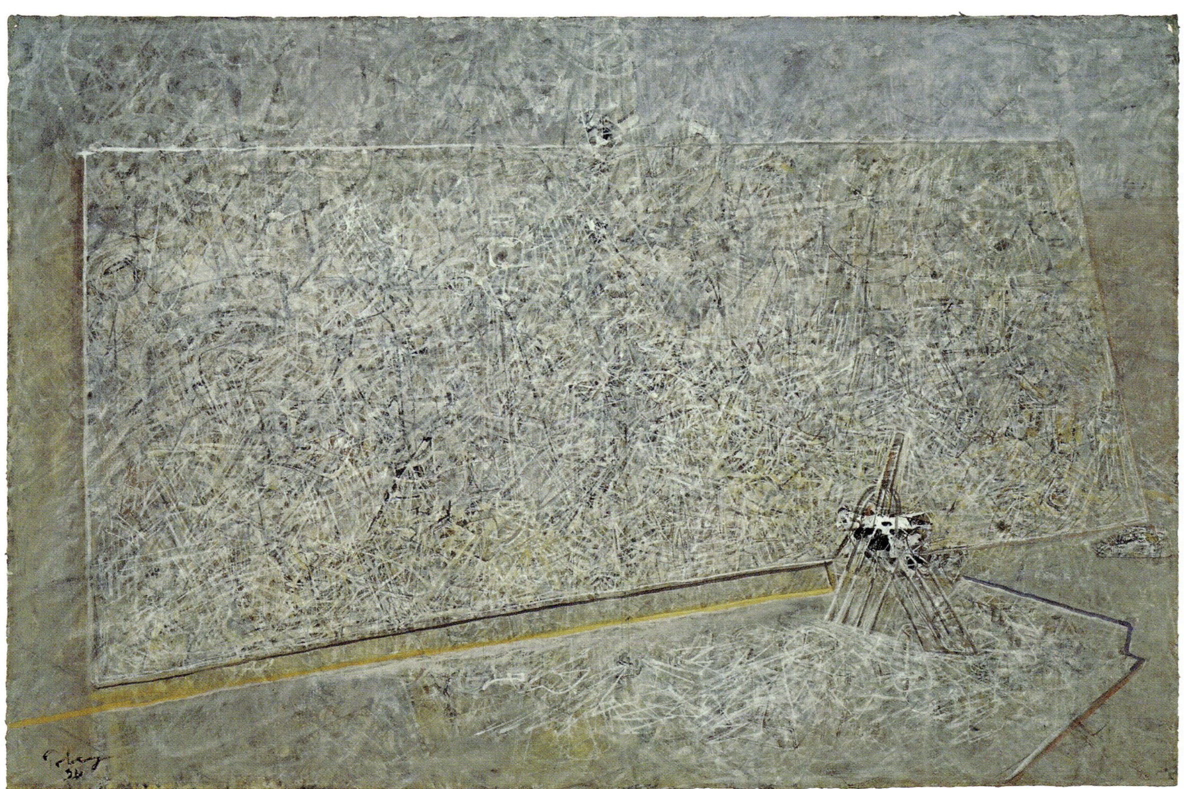

Mark Tobey (1890–1976)

Tozai, 1956
Tempera on oriental laid blue-gray paper mounted to paperboard
12 x 18¼ in. (30.5 x 46.4 cm)
Signed and dated lower left: *Tobey/56*
Gift of Ruth Carter Stevenson
1986.21

Mark Tobey's distinctive imagery reflects the artist's own system of personal beliefs, derived from a focused study of Eastern philosophy and religion. His beautiful and intricate works on paper function on multiple metaphorical levels; all express the concept of unity and a search for those commonalities that link mankind. Tobey created the tempera drawing *Tozai* following a return to Washington State from an extended period of travel in New York and Paris. In Seattle, which served as his primary residence for much of his career, the artist renewed his intensive study of Eastern religion in the company of Zen master Tamotsu Takizaki and Japanese-American artist Paul Horiuchi, both of whom shared Tobey's passionate interest in Asian art.

The title of this drawing carries several symbolic associations. The term *tozai* connotes the marriage of East and West, a harmonious concept that had been a cornerstone of the artist's personal philosophy following a trip to China and Japan in 1934. An outstanding example of his densely wrought drawings, *Tozai* likely was also a personal homage to the modest Horiuchi, who owned an antique shop by that name specializing in Asian antiques and whose own burgeoning artistic career Tobey earnestly encouraged. Tobey's close layering of expressive calligraphic strokes, known as "white writing," echoes Eastern brushwork and creates rich, yet subtle, spatial shifts on a minute scale, reflecting the Japanese appreciation for the larger universe as it is realized within the intimate and closely observed. This lively interplay of volume and line fuses the pictorial space; further three-dimensional illusion is suggested by the rigid linear forms that appear within the image. Tobey's animated interweaving of color and form also parallels the composition of classical music, to which he listened while painting, creating a synesthetic, symphonic whole comprised of many individual strands. Serene yet complex, his images are a lyrical visualization of Tobey's deeply felt spiritual convictions.

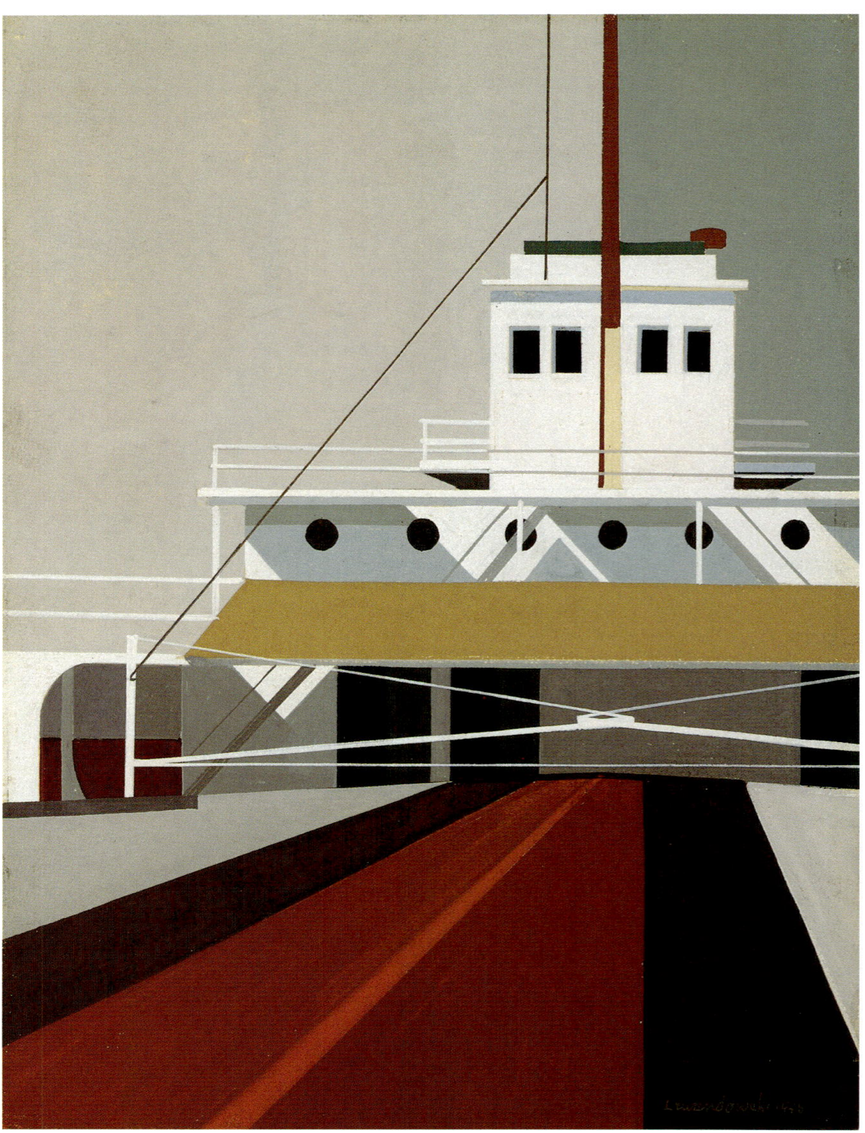

Edmund Lewandowski
(1914–1998)

Lake Freight, 1948
Opaque watercolor on wove, cream paper
11⅞ x 9⅛ in. (30.2 x 23.2 cm)
Signed and dated lower right: *Lewandowski 1948*
1985.4

Touchstones of American life outside the major urban areas of the Northeast informed a broad swath of American art during the 1930s and 1940s. A native of Milwaukee, Edmund Lewandowski adopted as his principal subject the industrial landscape of the Upper Midwest, an area where shipping and manufacturing were nourished by proximity to the nation's richest repository of iron ore around Lake Superior.

Before Lewandowski turned thirty, his work had been featured at leading museums in Paris, Chicago, New York, and Washington, D. C. His reputation rested on the clean lines and solid colors he used to vividly portray his home region's major industry. Lewandowski made *Lake Freight* in the year Wisconsin celebrated its centennial, while he was teaching at the Layton School of Art in his hometown. He had joined the faculty following his discharge from the U.S. Army Air Force, in which he had served from 1942 to 1946.

In *Lake Freight*, the vantage point from the stern of a massive freighter emphasizes the conjunction of its streamlined contours. A comparison with the similar but more highly detailed oil painting *Ore Freighter* (Milwaukee Art Museum) reveals how the artist distilled the ship to its most essential forms. The blue-gray shadows that fall across the ship's bridge conform to the rigid diagonal shapes of the vessel's angular and geometric contours. The long row of rectangular hatches spanning the length of the ship are reduced to unmodulated broad bands of rich color, with only slight exaggeration of the actual maritime palette. Lewandowski's emphasis on the simple beauty inherent in this indefatigable behemoth converted a utilitarian vessel of commerce into a cultural symbol of American technical ingenuity and economic power.

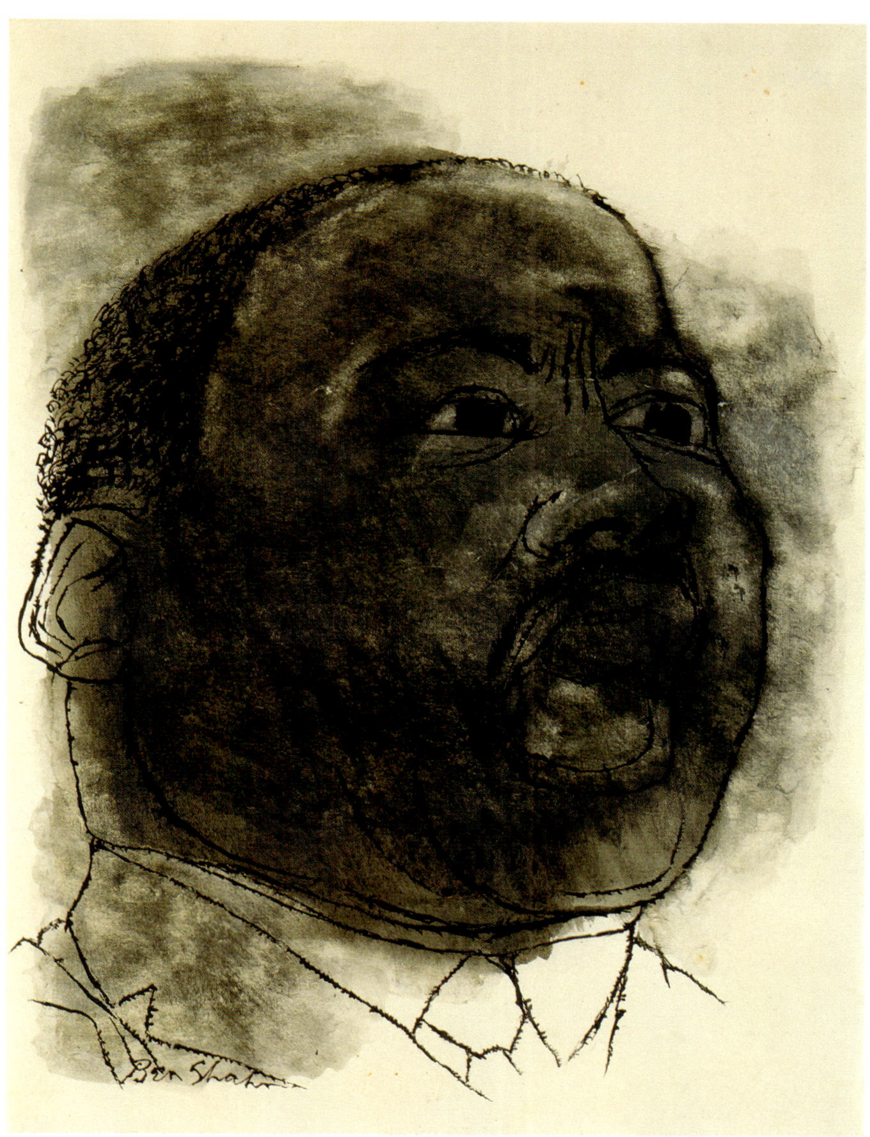

Ben Shahn
(1898–1969)

Martin Luther King, 1965
Ink and ink wash on oriental fibered cream paper
26¼ x 20⅜ in. (66.7 x 51.8 cm)
Signed lower left: *Ben Shahn*
1967.197

The volatile social issues that permeated the 1960s called for potent images commensurate with the country's uncertain mood. This wash drawing of civil rights leader Reverend Martin Luther King Jr. appeared on the cover of *Time* magazine on March 19, 1965, during one of the most emotionally fraught periods of the civil rights movement. On March 7 of that year, a day that swiftly gained notoriety as "Bloody Sunday," Alabama state troopers used billy clubs and tear gas to subdue over 500 demonstrators attempting a voting rights march in Selma. The violence continued two days later when a northern white clergyman was murdered after dining in a black-owned restaurant.

The editors of *Time* echoed the nationwide outrage in their extensive coverage of events unfolding in Selma, a community where the black population outnumbered the white, yet accounted for only one percent of registered voters. Ben Shahn's decision to accept the cover commission was consistent with the artist's own social activism, which dated back to the 1930s and included close involvement with the civil rights movement. Shahn believed portraiture should exceed mere physical documentation and reflect an individual's spiritual essence, and he gravitated to those subjects whose personal values paralleled his own.

Working swiftly to produce the drawing of King by the publication deadline, Shahn drew upon photographs of the minister that emphasized his powerful oratory. He portrayed King as a passionate, charismatic leader who, under the protection of the federal district court, would soon lead the march of some 25,000 protestors along the route from Selma to Montgomery as originally planned. King's ability to channel the groundswell of nonviolent protest resulted in the passage of the Voting Rights Act that August. The act was the federal government's pledge to enforce the Fifteenth Amendment, ratified in 1870, which guaranteed the right to vote regardless of race.

Further Readings about the Drawings and Watercolors Collection

Agee, William C. *Morton Livingston Schamberg (1881–1918): The Machine Pastels.* New York: Salander-O'Reilly Galleries, 1986.

Ahlborn, Richard E. *The San Antonio Missions: Edward Everett and the American Occupation, 1847.* Fort Worth: Amon Carter Museum in cooperation with Los Campadres de San Antonio Missions National Historical Park, 1985.

Balken, Deborah Bricker. *Arthur Dove: A Retrospective.* Andover, Mass.: Addison Gallery of American Art; Cambridge: MIT Press in association with Phillips Collection, 1997.

Baur, John I. H., and Margaret Conrads. *Meditations on Nature: The Drawings of David Johnson.* Yonkers, N.Y.: Hudson River Museum of Westchester, 1987.

Black, Mary. *Simplicity, A Grace: Jacob Maentel in Indiana.* Evansville, Ind.: Evansville Museum of Arts & Science, 1989.

Clark, Carol. *Thomas Moran: Watercolors of the American West.* Austin: University of Texas Press for Amon Carter Museum, 1980.

Clark, Carroll S., and Louise Heskett, eds. *Jan Matulka, 1890–1972.* Washington, D.C.: Smithsonian Institution Press for National Collection of Fine Arts and Whitney Museum of American Art, 1980.

DePietro, Anne Cohen. *Arthur Dove & Helen Torr: The Huntington Years.* Huntington, N.Y.: Heckscher Museum, 1989.

Ferber, Linda S. *William Trost Richards: American Landscape and Marine Painter, 1833–1905.* Brooklyn: Brooklyn Museum, 1973.

Ferber, Linda S., and William H. Gerdts. *The New Path: Ruskin and the American Pre-Raphaelites.* Brooklyn: Brooklyn Museum, 1985.

Fine, Ruth. *John Marin.* New York: Abbeville Press; Washington, D.C.: National Gallery of Art, 1990.

———. *O'Keeffe on Paper.* Santa Fe: Georgia O'Keeffe Museum; Washington, D.C.: National Gallery of Art, 2000.

Gilbert, Pamela. *Birds, Butterflies, and Other Wonders.* London: Merrell Holberton Publishers, 1998.

Haskell, Barbara. *Charles Demuth.* New York: Whitney Museum of American Art in association with Harry N. Abrams, 1987.

Hayes, Jeffrey. *Oscar Bluemner.* Cambridge and New York: Cambridge University Press, 1991.

Hill, May Brawley. *Fidelia Bridges: American Pre-Raphaelite.* New York: Berry-Hill Galleries, 1981.

Hobbs, Susan. *The Art of Thomas Wilmer Dewing: Beauty Reconfigured.* Brooklyn: Brooklyn Museum in association with Smithsonian Institution Press, 1996.

Huseman, Ben W. *Wild River, Timeless Canyons: Balduin Möllhausen's Watercolors of the Colorado.* Fort Worth: Amon Carter Museum, 1995.

Josephy, Alvin M., Jr. *The Artist Was a Young Man: The Life Story of Peter Rindisbacher.* Fort Worth: Amon Carter Museum, 1970.

Junker, Patricia, et al. *An American Collection: Works from the Amon Carter Museum.* New York: Hudson Hills Press in association with Amon Carter Museum, 2001.

Leith, Royal W. *A Quiet Devotion: The Life and Work of Henry Roderick Newman.* New York: Jordan-Volpe Gallery, 1996.

Lynes, Barbara Buhler. *Georgia O'Keeffe: Catalogue Raisonné.* Washington, D.C.: National Gallery of Art; Abiquiu, N. Mex.: Georgia O'Keeffe Foundation, 1999.

MacDonald, Margaret. *James McNeill Whistler: Drawings, Pastels, and Watercolours: A Catalogue Raisonné.* New Haven: Yale University Press for Paul Mellon Centre for Studies in British Art, 1995.

Moser, Joann. *Visual Poetry: The Drawings of Joseph Stella.* Washington, D.C.: Smithsonian Institution Press for National Museum of American Art, 1990.

Myers, Jane, and Tom Wolf. *The Shores of a Dream: Yasuo Kuniyoshi's Early Work in America.* Fort Worth: Amon Carter Museum, 1996.

Myers, Jane, ed. *Stuart Davis: Graphic Work and Related Paintings with a Catalogue Raisonné of the Prints.* Fort Worth: Amon Carter Museum, 1986.

Nesbett, Peter, ed. *The Complete Jacob Lawrence.* Seattle: University of Washington Press, 2001.

Rogers-Price, Vivian. *John Abbot in Georgia: The Vision of a Naturalist Artist (1751–ca. 1840).* Madison, Ga.: Madison-Morgan Cultural Center, 1983.

———. Introduction and Commentary to *John Abbot's Birds of Georgia: Selected Drawings from the Houghton Library, Harvard University.* Savannah: Beehive Foundation, 1997.

Sill, Gertrude. *John Haberle, Master of Illusion.* Springfield, Mass.: Museum of Fine Arts, 1985.

Simpson, Marc, Andrea Henderson, and Sally Mills. *Expressions of Place: The Art of William Stanley Haseltine.* San Francisco: Fine Arts Museums of San Francisco, 1992.

Townsend, J. Benjamin, ed. *Charles Burchfield's Journals: The Poetry of Place.* Albany: State University of New York Press, 1993.

Tyler, Ron. *Views of Texas, 1852–1856: Watercolors by Sarah Ann Lillie Hardinge.* Fort Worth: Amon Carter Museum, 1988.

———, ed. *Alfred Jacob Miller: Artist on the Oregon Trail.* Fort Worth: Amon Carter Museum, 1982.

Udall, Sharyn. *O'Keeffe and Texas.* San Antonio: Marion Koogler McNay Art Museum, 1998.

Weber, David J. *Richard H. Kern: Expeditionary Artist in the Far Southwest, 1848–1853.* Albuquerque: University of New Mexico Press for Amon Carter Museum, 1985.